ALIBABA'S WORLD

Prior to joining Alibaba.com in 2000, Porter Erisman worked for Ogilvy & Mather in Beijing. From 2000 to 2008, Porter worked as a Vice President at Alibaba.com and Alibaba Group, at various times leading the company's international website operations, international marketing, and corporate affairs as one of the company's first American employees. He is the writer/director of *Crocodile in the Yangtze*, a documentary about the rise of Alibaba and its famous founder, Jack Ma. He lives in Las Vegas.

ALIBABA'S WORLD

HOW A REMARKABLE CHINESE COMPANY IS CHANGING THE FACE OF GLOBAL BUSINESS

PORTER ERISMAN

MACMILLAN

First published in the United States 2015 by Palgrave Macmillan® Trade,
a division of St. Martin's Press LLC

First published in the UK 2015 by Macmillan
an imprint of Pan Macmillan, a division of Macmillan Publishers Limited
Pan Macmillan, 20 New Wharf Road, London N1 9RR
Basingstoke and Oxford
Associated companies throughout the world
www.panmacmillan.com

ISBN 978-1-4472-9064-3

Printed and bound by Gopsons Papers Ltd, Noida

Visit www.panmacmillan.com to read more about all our books
and to buy them. You will also find features, author interviews and
news of any author events, and you can sign up for e-newsletters
so that you're always first to hear about our new releases.

For Mom and Dad

CONTENTS

AUTHOR'S NOTE

MY GOAL WITH *ALIBABA'S WORLD* IS BOTH TO EDU-
cate and inspire. I hope that entrepreneurs and others chasing
a dream can read the book to learn from Alibaba's successes
and mistakes. And I hope that others can learn from Alibaba's story to better understand what it was like on the ground
during a transformative time when the Internet brought China
face-to-face with the West. In pursuit of this goal I've made every effort to present an accurate and authentic reflection of my
experiences.

Fortunately much of Alibaba's history was captured in the
200 hours of video archives that I gathered in preparing my
documentary, *Crocodile in the Yangtze*. This, and detailed
notes I took during my time at Alibaba, provided a valuable
reference for this book.

All the dialogue is based on actual conversations, but at
times I combine two separate conversations with one person
into one conversation. The same is true of some of Jack Ma's
early speeches where I have sometimes combined public comments he made separately at the time into one speech. I also

paraphrase Jack Ma's English occasionally to account for the fact that it is not his native language and sometimes includes small grammatical errors. In all cases I have made every effort to preserve the accuracy and authenticity of what was said by all parties.

In a few instances, when discussing confrontations or conflicts with former colleagues, I have left some minor characters unnamed. In a fast-growing start-up, there are always bumps and bruises, internal disagreements. However, my goal here is to use issues or conflicts as illustrations from which others may learn, not settle scores with individual colleagues. In the spirit of fairness, I also do my best to point out the times when I myself made mistakes or held the wrong assumptions.

This book was written independent of Alibaba, with no involvement by the company. Whether readers agree or disagree with my take on events, the opinions are entirely my own. It's my hope that sharing the story, in the most candid way possible, of how a schoolteacher rose from obscurity to build the world's largest e-commerce company can serve as a great case study for students, entrepreneurs, and anyone else setting out on a journey of their own.

INTRODUCTION

THE GREAT LEAPFROG FORWARD

NOVEMBER 7, 2006, WAS THE DAY I REALIZED THAT Alibaba had finally arrived. As I stood at the back of a packed auditorium at the Web 2.0 conference in San Francisco, my boss, Jack Ma, took the stage. With a typically entertaining speech he captivated the high-level audience, a who's who of the Internet world.

"I'm 100 percent 'made in China.' I learned English myself, and I know nothing about technology," Jack explained. "One of the reasons why Alibaba survived is because I know nothing about computers. I'm like a blind man riding on the back of a blind tiger."

As the audience laughed, I noticed someone crouched down in the back of the auditorium, scribbling down every word Jack said. Curious, I leaned over to see who was so intent on transcribing Jack's speech. I was shocked to find it was Jeff Bezos, the founder and CEO of Amazon.

Bezos—the father of e-commerce—eager to learn from Alibaba? This was the man who had pioneered e-commerce and grown Amazon.com into an Internet behemoth. This was the entrepreneur named *Time* magazine's Person of the Year back in 1999 when Alibaba was still an obscure start-up in Jack Ma's apartment. Bezos was a business leader we had always looked up to and admired—not to mention borrowed ideas from. And now he was borrowing ours!

Jeff continued taking notes as Jack spoke to the rapt group.

"Believe in your dreams, find good people, and make sure the customer is happy. I see a lot of US companies sending professional managers to China. They are making their boss in the US happy but not the Chinese customer."

Jack had always wanted to meet Jeff Bezos, so I leaned over, introduced myself, and gave Jeff my card. Jeff said he'd love to meet Jack as well. After Jack's speech the two of us met with Jeff in the convention center lobby. With his trademark laugh and infectious enthusiasm, Jeff commended Jack on his speech: "You made some great points up there, Jack! I'd love for you to visit us in Seattle someday." As Jeff walked away, Jack and I beamed like two starstruck groupies in a garage band who'd just been validated by their favorite rock star.

Seven months later I picked up the *Wall Street Journal* to find an interview with Jeff, who was announcing an expansion in China. He described how he was determined to avoid the problems other foreign Internet companies had encountered in China, explaining that the reason they struggled was "because the Chinese management team is busy trying to keep their American bosses happy, instead of trying to keep their Chinese customers happy. And that's a mistake we will not make." Yes—it seemed Jeff had learned something from Jack.

Little did Jack and I know that in just a few years, Alibaba's sales volume would surpass those of both our idols—Amazon *and* eBay. Combined. Not just in China. Everywhere.

When Alibaba got started in Jack Ma's apartment, it seemed far-fetched to think that Western Internet companies would someday be learning from China's e-commerce founders. With only two million Internet users in China, less than 1 percent of the country's population was online. And of that 1 percent, even fewer would consider purchasing something online. The barriers were simply too great. Consumer purchasing power was too low. Credit card penetration was negligible. Logistics infrastructure was primitive. It was unclear whether the government would embrace or reject the Internet. And e-commerce seemed impossible in the context of China's Wild West capitalism, where scammers were all too common and where buyers and sellers who had never met in person simply didn't trust each other enough to do transactions online.

Fast-forward 15 years, and the difference in the numbers is astounding. Alibaba now has approximately 300 million customers and executes about 80 percent of China's e-commerce transactions. More than half of all packages shipped in China are from deals that originated on Alibaba's websites. And during its 2014 Singles' Day promotion—a shopping holiday that Alibaba invented—Alibaba's consumer shopping websites handled $9.3 billion in transactions on just one day—more than the total US online sales on Black Friday and Cyber Monday combined. All this in a country where the per capita income is just $6,800 per year and only about 25 percent of the population has ever shopped online. Compared to the United States, China's e-commerce boom is just beginning.

Alibaba's experience has shown that, although e-commerce was slower to take off in China than in the West, when it did take root, it was far more important to the overall economy. In just 15 years China's e-commerce infrastructure has leapfrogged its Western counterparts' and is introducing entirely new ways of doing business. China has become a dynamic laboratory for e-commerce innovations, with important lessons for businesses everywhere.

Alibaba is also branching out into a number of entirely new frontiers, well beyond traditional e-commerce. Within a year of launching its first money market fund, Alibaba's finance unit was operating one of China's top funds, with over $90 billion under management. It has started a movie studio to produce original content. Will Alibaba someday realize its goal of becoming China's largest bank? Will it give Fox and Disney a run for their money in film production?

The scale of Alibaba's growth grabbed the business world's attention when it went public on September 19, 2014. Alibaba's was the largest IPO (initial public offering) in history, dominated global business headlines, and made Alibaba the most valuable e-commerce company in the world. And Jack, who began his career making less than $20 per month, was suddenly worth $19.5 billion soon after the IPO.

This book is the inside story of how all this happened. How a schoolteacher and 17 of his friends rose from obscurity and overcame immense obstacles to build an e-commerce powerhouse that is transforming global business.

The founding of Alibaba was really the birth of e-commerce in China. From 2000 to 2008, I worked at Alibaba as a vice president in a variety of roles as the company grew from a small apartment into the behemoth it is today. I'll chronicle both the successes and missteps the company made on the road to riches. In the process I hope to explain how Chinese e-commerce got to where it is today, where things are headed, and what it means for the global marketplace.

After leaving Alibaba in 2008, I produced and directed *Crocodile in the Yangtze,* an independent documentary film about my experience. The film premiered at the Sonoma International Film Festival in April 2012, and I subsequently spent two years traveling the world to show the film to festival audiences, students, and entrepreneurs. The journey took me to more than 50 cities on six continents—from Silicon Valley to Bangalore to Nigeria and just about everywhere in between. It taught me that the Alibaba story, so multifaceted, has universal appeal, and from each Q&A session I got a greater sense of which aspects people in different places were interested in. The plucky start-up spirit that challenged eBay and Amazon when they ruled the e-commerce roost? The rise of a schoolteacher from the far-flung provinces to economic royalty in what is still a Communist country? Or the seismic shifting of the world's attention from West to East?

My time at Alibaba challenged a number of my assumptions about business and life. My experience was a positive one overall, and this memoir reflects that. I saw a company grow from a small apartment into China's first global Internet company, battling—and beating—eBay in China along the way. And I saw a team of ordinary people come together to build a company that has fundamentally reshaped the way people do business in China and beyond. But the goal of this book is not simply to say that Alibaba is great or that Jack Ma is a hero. It is simply to answer this question: What made Alibaba so successful where so many of its competitors failed?

After 15 years the Alibaba story is, in many ways, still just beginning. And how it ends is up to Jack and a new team of colleagues—and how well they adhere to the values that have carried them this far. Alibaba is no longer a David. It is a Goliath. And as a Goliath it will face an entirely new set of challenges. But whether Alibaba ultimately succeeds or fails, its rise remains one of the most fascinating and instructive business stories of our time. By sharing my experience at the company as candidly as possible, I hope that entrepreneurs or others setting out on a similar journey may gain some inspiration and avoid some mistakes. It is my sincere belief that the spread of e-commerce, and the grassroots economic opportunities it provides, can transform the lives of millions, if not billions, of people around the world.

THE RIGHT PERSON

@ THE RIGHT PLACE

@ THE RIGHT TIME

I SLID INTO THE BACKSEAT OF THE TAXI AS THE driver dropped the meter's flag and turned to me. "So where you headed?"

"Wensan road. Alibaba headquarters."

We bumped along the Hangzhou streets for a bit, past construction sites, shops, and Hangzhou's West Lake. Then the driver struck up a conversation.

"Do you work at Alibaba?"

"Yes, I joined the company in 2000. I've worked there for about six years now," I said.

"Oh, really? I didn't know Alibaba had foreigners. So why did you decide to work in a Chinese company?"

"I thought it would be more fun to help a Chinese company go global than to help a foreign company enter China. It's an exciting challenge."

The driver hesitated a bit and then went on.

"I actually know Jack Ma. We were in grade school together. The same class. Do you work with him much?"

"Yeah, we work closely together. I've traveled with him to a lot of different countries."

"Do you want to know why Jack Ma is so successful today?" he asked.

Hmm. I wasn't sure I wanted to know where the guy was heading, but I let him go on.

"It's because he's lucky. He was at the right place at the right time."

Having seen all of the hard work that Jack and his team had put into building Alibaba, I tried to resist getting defensive. If building China's largest e-commerce company was just a matter of being at the right place at the right time, I thought, why didn't 1.3 billion other people in China see and grab the same opportunity when the Internet came to China? And if the driver and Jack were classmates in the same city, wouldn't the driver have been at the right place at the right time as well?

But I kept mum, because I didn't see any point in debating him. Yes, Jack had been in the right *place* at the right *time*. But on paper millions of other people were more qualified to start an e-commerce business than a schoolteacher from Hangzhou who twice failed his college entrance exams. Yet Jack was the only one who seized the moment. He was the right *person* at the right *place* at the right *time*.

So why Jack? What made him different? What motivated him? In many ways the answer lies in his life before Alibaba, a story I heard in bits and pieces over the years.

Jack was born on September 10, 1964, just two years before Mao's Cultural Revolution. Jack's early years were no doubt shaped by the political turmoil that marked the period from 1966 to 1976, a time when intellectuals, artists, and capitalists were tormented by round after round of class warfare. As the grandson of a landlord and son of a performer of Pingtan—a traditional folk art combining music with storytelling—Jack was on the wrong side of history in the eyes of the Communists. This led to Jack's being bullied by classmates, and his frequent fights got him into trouble at his school and with his parents.

Perhaps as an escape Jack spent his free time absorbed in martial arts novels. He started with the Chinese classics and then moved on to the contemporary writer Louis Cha, whose popular *wuxia* (martial arts and chivalry) novels told tales of noble warriors defending the common people and underdogs using their wits—rather than brute strength—to defeat more powerful opponents.

The martial arts stories may have helped Jack overcome the first thing anyone ever notices about him—his appearance. Alternately described as elfish and impish by the media, Jack's diminutive figure brought him unwanted attention and ridicule. Even within his own family he was sometimes teased as being the runt. When introducing his three kids, his dad was known to joke, "And this one we found in the garbage."

You'd think being teased about his appearance and bullied by peers would destroy a young person's confidence. But in Jack's case it somehow gave him strength. As China opened after Mao's death, foreigners began to trickle into Jack's home town of Hangzhou to visit West Lake. When Jack's middle school geography teacher told him that she'd seen foreigners near the lake, Jack became curious and went down to see for himself. He soon made a daily habit of pedaling his bicycle to the lake to befriend foreign tourists and practice English with them.

Jack developed a relationship with one Australian family in particular with whom he bonded over a game of Frisbee. They remained pen pals for many years. Through his relationship with the Australian family, Jack first traveled out of China, which he said "showed me that everything I had learned about the outside world in my Chinese textbooks was wrong." The family became such a strong influence on Jack that he described the family's father as "like a father to me."

Jack's many friendships with foreigners improved his English well beyond his contemporaries' in Hangzhou while also opening his mind to international thinking. So he was a natural candidate to become an English teacher. Despite failing his college entrance exams twice because of his struggles with math, Jack finally entered the Hangzhou Normal University, a teachers' college, where he was elected president of his class.

After graduation he began work as an English teacher at a local university, where he made $12 per month. Most Chinese teachers required rote learning from textbooks, but Jack taught extemporaneously, straying from the texts and relying on storytelling and humor to engage his students. He incorporated in his lessons a bit of showmanship learned from his performer father, and Jack became a favorite teacher on campus.

After fulfilling a commitment he had made to a mentor to serve as an English teacher for five years, Jack decided it was time to "jump into the sea" and start a business. "Everything I taught my students was from books," he said. "I wanted to get some real-life experience. Whether I succeeded or failed was not important. Because I knew I could always take that experience back to share with my students."

Jack's first venture was the Hangzhou Hope Translation Agency, which he started in 1994 to serve the growing number of local businesses engaged in tourism and foreign trade. As Jack became known around Hangzhou for his English skills and ability to communicate with foreigners, local government officials asked him to travel to the United States to try to sort out a dispute they were having with a US partner who had promised to fund the construction of a toll highway.

Jack flew to the United States with high hopes, but when he arrived in Los Angeles, he began to suspect that the man he'd been sent to meet was a con man. His fears were heightened when his host flashed a gun and then left Jack stranded without a car in a Malibu mansion for a couple days to stew about whether or not he would report back to the Chinese partner that everything on the US side of the deal was on the up and up. Terrified and suspecting his US host was hiding important information from the Chinese partner, Jack eventually made his way to Seattle, where he had American friends.

In Seattle Jack's friends introduced him to the Internet by sitting him down in front of a computer for the first time. "I was afraid to touch the computer, such an expensive thing. But they told me, 'Jack—go ahead. It's not a bomb!' So I typed in the word *beer*, B-E-E-R, and I could see German beer, Japanese beer, but no Chinese beer. So I searched the word *China* and the response was 'no results.' So I said to myself, *This is something interesting. If we can take companies in China and make a home page for them, this could be something big.*"

When Jack returned to China, he set up China's first Internet company, China Pages, a sort of online English-language directory for Chinese companies and information. Unfortunately Hangzhou did not yet have Internet access. So the businesses he initially targeted as prospective clients reacted as if he were trying to sell them magic beans. Once he finally did make sales, he had to gather the client company's information and have it couriered to his friends in Seattle, who would build a web page. To prove that Jack's website existed, the Seattle friends would print out the pages and courier a copy to China for Jack to present to the customers.

China Pages had some early success and soon caught the eye of the state-run Hangzhou Telecom, which had started its own rival service. Fearing he might have to compete against a government-backed player, Jack decided the only way to survive would be to team up with Hangzhou Telecom. They formed a joint venture, but Jack soon found himself at odds with Hangzhou Telecom's management and left in frustration.

Next he headed to Beijing, where he worked at a company started under the Ministry of Foreign Trade and Economic Cooperation (MOFTEC). Thinking he could help pioneer e-commerce from within the government, he took charge of an organization designed to help small- and medium-sized enterprises take advantage of the Internet. But once again Jack felt stifled by the government bureaucrats ultimately responsible for the organization. "My boss wanted to use the Internet to control small businesses, but I wanted to use the Internet to empower small businesses. We had a totally different philosophy."

Finally, as China's own Internet boom began to take off in 1999, Jack gathered the friends he had dragged to Beijing to work on his team at MOFTEC and told them he had a new idea for a venture—Alibaba. He had learned from the ups and downs of his experiences with China Pages and the government. Jack now had a clearer vision for how e-commerce could finally take root in China. He'd chosen the name Alibaba because it was a globally recognized story and conjured up images of small businesses saying "open sesame" to new treasures and opportunities through the Internet. Thus Alibaba was born.

Which brings us to early 2000. . . .

BOOM!

I'll see you in Shanghai. Let's go have some fun!!!!

—Jack

IT WAS THE FIRST EMAIL I EVER GOT FROM JACK. The one-line delivery sounded more like a kid on his way to Disneyland than the CEO of a company that had just raised $25 million from Goldman Sachs and Japan's Softbank. But the playful tone didn't surprise me, given the spirit of the times. After all, it was March 2000 and a great time to be alive—if you were involved in the Internet industry in China.

During the previous five years those of us working in China could only watch with envy as friends and former classmates took part in the thrilling US Internet boom. As companies like Yahoo!, Amazon, and eBay became listed on Nasdaq, wave after wave of Internet mania spread throughout Europe and the United States, minting thousands of fresh millionaires with each new IPO. But with less than 1 percent of the country's population online, China's Internet industry seemed destined to languish for decades.

Everything changed in the summer of 1999, with the IPO of China.com, a Hong Kong–based consumer Internet portal that styled itself as the "Yahoo! of China." Never mind that it was a hollow company with no real business model. China.com had a great domain name and appealed to investors chasing China's 2.6 billion eyeballs. Just as Netscape's IPO had triggered the Internet gold rush in the United States, China.com's IPO sent investors rushing to China. And for those of us patiently waiting for the Internet mania to arrive, it was a welcome stampede.

At the time I was working as the head of a technology group at Ogilvy & Mather in Beijing, managing PR and marketing campaigns for foreign companies entering the China market. When I first took the role at Ogilvy, I had assumed that I'd be helping grow the business of multinational companies like Nokia, our largest tech client at the time. But as the Internet boom took hold, my client list quickly grew to include an increasing number of foreign Internet companies that showed an interest in China. Not long after the US companies started entering the China market, homegrown startups emerged, modeling themselves after their US counterparts. Within a year, the number of Internet clients in my group had grown from one to ten. I watched these clients not only having a lot of fun but discovering the possibility of changing the world along the way. I was beginning to think it was time to join a start-up myself.

Little did I know, while I was toiling away in Beijing, that Jack Ma and a team of his friends were secretly working day and night in a small apartment in Hangzhou, two hours south of Shanghai. While other companies in China were chasing consumers, creating Chinese clones of the hottest US properties,

Jack and his team set out to capture businesses. Their vision was to build a marketplace connecting the world's small- and medium-sized businesses engaged in global trade—the "widget economy" made up of manufacturers, trading companies, and wholesalers comprising the global supply chain. And their website—Alibaba.com—was meant to allow these small businesses access to the riches that only the Internet could unlock.

In October 1999 Alibaba finally came out of hiding and was officially launched at a press conference in Hong Kong, where Jack also announced a $5 million round of investment in Alibaba led by Goldman Sachs. Word began to spread as news stories trickled out about a little-known schoolteacher who was trying to build a platform for global trade. In January 2000 Jack and his team raised another $20 million, led by Japan's Softbank. And by March, in preparation for the company's global expansion, Alibaba began to hire a professional international management team.

At about this time I started looking for a start-up to join. But my hunt for the next big thing got off to a slow start.

I started with an interview with a leading Internet portal. I met with the vice president of marketing, a transplant from Hong Kong who was hiring a corporate communications manager in preparation for a possible IPO.

"I think it would be exciting to work with the team to help craft the vision for you and the company as it moves forward," I told my would-be boss.

"Let's be clear here. I'll set the vision and you execute it," he coldly replied.

With that I scratched them off the list. I was looking to join a team, not a dictatorship.

I next interviewed with an online stock trading company that billed itself as the "E-Trade of China." But when I met with the husband-and-wife team who had founded the company, something didn't smell right. Their company headquarters was a virtual office. And the sources of their investment seemed suspect. By the end of the interview I was convinced all they wanted was a Western face for their company as they pursued activities of questionable legality.

Finally I interviewed with a Taiwanese e-commerce company called pAsia that operated an online consumer auction website in mainland China. The company was gearing up for an IPO and had invested in an expensive corporate identity and logo design based on the name eAsia. But when its executives learned that the name eAsia was already registered by a company in Central Asia, the Taiwanese company changed its name to pAsia to avoid redesigning the logo. This might have been fine if, when pronounced in Chinese, the letter *P* wasn't a homonym for *fart*.

ON THE SIDELINES of an Internet conference, I told a friend about the difficulties I was having finding a start-up to join. Even if the company had a good business model, I explained, the management styles seemed too top-down and regimented.

"Oh, I didn't even know you were looking. I should introduce you to Alibaba. They are trying to build China's first global Internet company and are looking for someone to manage their international PR. You'd be based in Hong Kong but traveling to Europe, the US, and all around Asia."

My eyes lit up. I'd known many US Internet companies that were coming into the China market and many Chinese companies that were trying to become a local Internet giant. But I had never heard of a Chinese Internet company that wanted to go global. It was about as big a dream as one could have, and the challenge appealed to me. Plus, I liked the idea of being based in China but traveling worldwide. Even if Alibaba failed, I thought, surely more Chinese companies will be going global, and the skills would be great to have.

"Alibaba's just raised a lot of money, and it's building an international team. You should give them a look," my friend advised.

A few weeks later I flew to Shanghai to meet Jack and his team. We attended a customer gathering Alibaba had organized to celebrate the opening of its new Shanghai office. As a taxi took me along the overhead expressway to the Galaxy Hotel, the Shanghai skyline whizzed by. The entire town seemed to be under construction; cranes adorned the sites of new skyscrapers and office buildings everywhere. Silicon Valley may be booming, I thought, but that was nothing compared to the changes going on in China.

I wasn't sure what to expect at the party. I exchanged business cards with a few of the Alibaba members, manufacturers engaged in a range of businesses I didn't really understand, such as petrochemical fiber, ball bearings, and all sorts of widgets. There was an awkwardness in the room as people stood around waiting to see what would happen next. Then the doors burst open and Jack Ma strolled into the room, followed by an eager entourage of young staff members. After shaking hands with some of the Alibaba members who had assembled, Jack jumped on the stage and began to address the crowd.

"Thanks for coming, everyone. Although we see you online all the time, nothing replaces meeting face to face. Tonight I want to lay out our vision. From the first day we started Alibaba, we had three main goals. We want Alibaba to be one of the top ten websites in the world. We want Alibaba to be a partner to all businesspeople. And we want to build a company that lasts 80 years!"

As Jack addressed the crowd, he seemed distracted by a blinding spotlight and jumped around from topic to topic. Although he clearly had vision and ambition, it felt a bit like watching a first-time performance of a rock star wannabe at an open mic night. The crowd was growing impatient. One of the expats at my table leaned over and said to me, "They could use someone like you at this company; these guys need some help."

Jack wrapped up his speech, receiving a smattering of applause. Although the event wasn't a slick production, the innocence of it appealed to me. Unlike a lot of the other companies I had interviewed with, Jack and his team seemed to be driven by more than just money. It seemed like a fun adventure. Shortly after the speech Jack's assistant motioned for me to come over and sat me down with Jack.

"That was a great speech, Jack," I said, being generous to the man who might be my future boss.

"Actually my performance wasn't that great tonight," he replied. "The lights were in my eyes the whole time."

He asked me a few simple questions and then, with a smile on his face and glint in his eye, he said, "I've heard a lot of great things about you. So when are you joining us?"

I guessed he hadn't even seen my resume. We spoke for only about five minutes before he offered me a job. It was clear that Jack was someone who made decisions quickly, based on instinct and gut. But he had a sort of mischievous charm about him—I could tell that whether Alibaba failed or succeeded, working for him would be a great adventure.

I was invited to drinks at the Hard Rock Cafe with a group of expat managers who had recently been hired from a number of big-name companies, including McKinsey, American Express, and Oracle. They had given up their large expat compensation packages for a chance to join the dot-com dream. With the euphoria of the Internet in the air, we drank and chanted "A-li-ba-ba, A-li-ba-ba" all night and bar-hopped around Shanghai.

I woke up the next morning with a wicked hangover and stumbled down to the lobby for a meeting with Alibaba's CFO, Joe Tsai. A graduate of both Yale undergrad and Yale law school, Joe had given up a high-paying finance job to join Alibaba in October of the previous year. He was sharp, composed, and had a strong sense of purpose. With bloodshot eyes and a queasy stomach, I tried to maintain a professional posture as Joe began speaking.

"Everyone is really impressed with you, and we'd love for you to join our team. We're prepared to offer you a position, with a salary of $100,000 per year, plus stock options." I gulped and tried my best to stay calm. The amount was about 50 percent more than my current salary.

I wanted the job. But with my best attempt at a poker face, I bluffed, "Hmm . . . I'm pretty happy with where I am now. I'm going to have to think about it."

"Well, you should consider that we are planning to go public in about three months. Based on current valuations that we are being given by Goldman Sachs, your stock options would be worth $1 million when we IPO."

I gulped again. One million dollars? All I ever wanted was enough money to put a roof over my head and have time to travel, and this would make it possible. Could I actually become a millionaire in just three months?

A few days later I signed my contract and prepared to move to Hong Kong. With a month between jobs I decided to take a couple weeks to lie on the beach in the Philippines and relish the new opportunity ahead. Not only would I have a new job I loved, but I also might get rich along the way.

Before I left, I sat down at my computer and pulled up a blank Excel file. At the top of the spreadsheet I typed "Countdown to Millionaire" and saw that I'd be able to retire in just four years, once all my stock options had vested. But of course the stock market had other ideas.

BUST

I UNPACKED MY FLIP-FLOPS AND SUNSCREEN AND settled into my beachfront hotel room in the Philippines. Outside I could hear the waves crashing as music drifted in from the beachfront bar. After a year of being at the beck and call of my clients in Beijing, I could finally enjoy a guilt-free vacation, with no projects hanging over my head or client calls to disturb my peace. There was only the shining promise of the next exciting chapter in my career and life.

Before heading out to the beach for a sunset drink, I decided to turn on CNBC to see the latest news about Internet stocks. Crash! Bust! It was clear that the market correction that had begun in March 2000 was continuing into April, creating a Wall Street train wreck.

"The Nasdaq tumbles for a fifth day in a row. . . . Stocks headed lower again. . . . More troubles for tech. . . ."

For the next few days I hardly left my room. My eyes were glued to the TV screen. And as the ticker scrolled relentlessly, I watched my Internet dreams slowly fade away.

THE FOREIGN EXPERTS

I STOOD AT THE BASE OF HONG KONG'S CITIBANK Tower and scanned up the building until its glassy facade met the clouds. It was a far cry from the dusty streets of Beijing, where I'd been living in a drab Communist apartment block on the city's outskirts and scrimping to save enough money to pay off my business school loans. Although I'd come to like the gritty vibe of Beijing, moving to Hong Kong to join Alibaba was a welcome return to the modernity and convenience of a global business center.

As I walked into the building, I felt a bit like a kid on the first day of high school. I was excited to start something new but wondered how I'd fit in with the big kids. I'd been working for two years in Beijing and had gotten used to mainland China's raw form of entrepreneurship, which stood in stark contrast to Hong Kong's polish and style. This was the big leagues.

When I reached the twenty-eighth floor, I strolled down the quiet hall and buzzed my way into Alibaba's new offices. In the corner office I found Todd Daum, my new boss and Alibaba's vice president of marketing. Even though I hadn't known Todd before joining the company, I felt a certain level of familiarity with him; he had a marketing background and was a fellow alum of the MBA program at Northwestern's Kellogg School of Management.

"Welcome aboard," said Todd, shaking my hand before leading me through the office. "We've already got a lot of big things brewing, and we're happy you are here to get started on them." Working for Todd was one of the reasons I'd joined Alibaba. Unlike the dictatorial managers I'd encountered in my interviews at Chinese Internet start-ups, Todd was down to earth, friendly, and seemed willing to include me in the marketing team's strategic decisions. Before joining Alibaba he had worked at American Express, and I saw him as having a lot of experience, someone I could learn from.

After chatting with Todd, I was introduced to the newly hired executive team, made up of international managers with a dazzling mix of pedigrees from the world's top universities, consulting firms, and investment banks. It was clear that Jack Ma had assembled his dream team, and I had no doubt that the management section of our IPO prospectus would be attractive to any investor.

I took my seat in a cluster of cubicles in the office's interior, a sort of kids' table for the senior and middle managers. It was perfectly fine—this hodgepodge group seemed like a lot of fun. There was David Oliver, a former New Zealand sheep farmer who had somehow found his way into China's tech scene, working for a start-up in Beijing before joining Alibaba in its Hangzhou apartment as one of the company's first Westerners. Then there was Brian Wong, a Chinese American who'd been working as an assistant to San Francisco mayor Willie Brown before joining Alibaba as a business development manager. And Brian's good friend and former classmate, Emily Fong Mitchell, a Hawaiian with a sunny personality and sharp wit who worked with me on the marketing team. While our kids' table lacked professional experience, we quickly formed a common bond over the hardship and adventure of having previously studied and lived in mainland China.

After settling in, I sat down for a meeting with Todd. "So what's the status of the IPO?" I asked, wondering if it was still on track. "Things have changed," Todd said. "It doesn't look like we'll be having an IPO any time soon. Not in this market."

With these words I realized I'd have to recalibrate my expectations. Many things had attracted me to Alibaba. The adventure. The possibility of changing the world. The chance to pioneer something new. But if I'm totally honest with myself, the idea of becoming a millionaire didn't hurt. Now that my "Countdown to Millionaire" timeline had been extended indefinitely, I'd have to get my motivation from these other goals.

It was nice to meet the people I'd be working with in Hong Kong, but I was also curious about the team on the mainland. "So when are we going up to Hangzhou to see the headquarters and meet the team up there?" I asked Todd.

"To be honest I don't see much point in going up there anymore. Since I joined the company, the marketing team there has kind of stopped listening to us here in Hong Kong, and they've started to do their own thing. Look, this is what they're coming up with for ads," he said, pointing to an online banner ad. Typical of Chinese websites at the time, it had a bunch of flashy animations and lacked the familiar minimalist qualities of Western sites like Yahoo!.

I had to admit that the ad looked amateurish. But more discouraging than the unprofessionalism of the ad was how Todd responded to my question. It seemed a divide already was forming between the Hangzhou and international management teams. And rather than trying to address it, Todd seemed to already be giving up.

Because I had spent several years working in China, I knew just how important it was to gain the friendship and trust of one's local colleagues. In my first job after business school I learned this lesson the hard way. I had been put in charge of marketing a children's candy line at a multinational company in Beijing, and it had been a disaster. I focused plenty of time on developing a great marketing strategy but not enough time on winning the confidence and support of my local colleagues. Eight months later I left the company because I had failed to fit in with management. In a Chinese company, I'd learned, the informal structure was just as important as the organizational chart. And before you could focus on strategy, it was important to get to know your teammates.

"Okay, it sounds like the situation might be a bit frustrating right now," I said, "but at some point I'd like to get to Hang-zhou to get to know the team a bit."

"I don't think that's really the priority right now," he said. "But if you have a business reason to go up there, then it would make sense."

Later that week David Oliver gave me a heads-up that Jack was coming to Hong Kong. "Porter, now that you're running Alibaba's PR, I should let you know that there's a big event arranged for Jack later this week here in Hong Kong. It should be huge, with a lot of media."

I was new to the Hong Kong Internet scene and curious to see how it compared to Beijing's. When I arrived at the event, the difference struck me immediately. Beijing's Internet industry had been built from the ground up by entrepreneurs from humble backgrounds with little business experience. Unlike the state-owned enterprises that dominated the rest of the Chinese economy, the Internet industry was a meritocracy, where good ideas, hard work, and innovation meant much more than having the right contacts. (Especially since it was so new that you hardly knew who the right contacts were.)

However, Hong Kong's "new economy" seemed to be dominated by the sons and daughters of a handful of established tycoons. As I walked around the room exchanging cards, people chatted less about their company's vision or business models and more about which tycoon was backing it or how much money they'd just raised. With cocktails flowing and people dressed in expensive suits and party dresses, it felt more like a movie premiere than a gathering of tech start-ups.

Nevertheless Jack Ma's first speaking event in Hong Kong had attracted a huge audience. In a city where money talks, Alibaba's having raised $25 million from leading investors was enough to bring out the Internet industry in full force. Dressed more casually than most of the other partygoers, Jack arrived and slowly worked his way through the crowd, set apart by his diminutive figure and elfin features. After being introduced by the event's organizer, Jack took the stage:

> It is exciting to be here in Hong Kong because we are growing our international office here a lot and putting together a really great management team. Hong Kong is great because there

are so many professional managers. And almost all my co-founders back in Hangzhou have no business experience. So I told my founders that they shouldn't expect to be the senior managers in the company. We need to find those experts who have real business experience to take the company to the next level. You see, I was trained as an English teacher. So I know nothing about running a company. And after four years I will resign as CEO and hand over the company to a new generation of managers.

It seemed a mature point of view—he recognized his limitations and those of his cofounders and knew when to pass the baton. Jack continued: "So what is Alibaba? I remember I gave a talk in Singapore, and the topic was e-commerce in Asia. And I looked around the panel, and all of the speakers were from the USA. And I thought that Asia is Asia and America is America. Asia has its own way of doing e-commerce. So our goal with Alibaba is to be the top business-to-business [B2B] marketplace in the world. We will combine Asian wisdom and Western operations."

The crowd clapped, both inspired and entertained. People were starting to warm up to Jack.

"Business-to-business websites in the West go after the big companies, the whales. But in Asia commerce is dominated by the shrimp. So we are going after the shrimp. It's easy to catch a shrimp. But if you try to catch a whale, you might get hurt."

The crowd laughed. A hand went up in the audience. It belonged to an analyst from a major investment bank.

"That's great, Jack, but what's your revenue model?"

"Well, there are a lot of ways we can make money someday. But right now our website is totally free, because we want to attract new members. Once our members make money, we will make money."

"But you didn't answer my question," the analyst followed up. "How will you make money?"

"If I told you, I'd have to kill you," Jack joked. Both laughter and snickering followed his remark. Yes, Jack was funny. But he was trying to convince an audience full of investors and bankers that they shouldn't be thinking about making a profit at this point.

"We will make lots of money someday," Jack continued. "But right now we are running too fast for revenues."

The day after the event my colleagues in the Hong Kong office passed along an article that appeared on a leading industry news site, Internet.com: "Alibaba Running Too Fast for Revenues, Says CEO Ma." In an era when dot-coms were coming under increasing pressure to generate revenues, the highly critical article was not well received. And as the head of PR I was the first to hear about it.

"Porter, what is this?" one of the newly hired directors asked. She had just left a major investment bank and generous compensation package to join Alibaba and didn't seem amused by her new boss' style. "We really need to move beyond the Jack Ma story. He was a great founder, but we really can't have him talking the way he does. No one will ever take us seriously. We're supposed to be a business-to-business marketplace."

Another manager pulled me aside. "It's really time for Alibaba to get Jack out of the spotlight and get the focus on our other, more seasoned, managers. Jack is totally off-message." There seemed to be a growing consensus among many of the newly hired Hong Kong executives that our own CEO was bad for our image. I thought it strange, but not too surprising, that some of the expat staff wanted to take charge and have the management handed over to them sooner rather than later. They had always worked for multinationals and were used to managing the local staff, not the other way around. But in this case people seemed to be forgetting who had hired whom.

The comments from my colleagues were the second sign of a small fracture between the Hong Kong senior managers and the founding team in Hangzhou—a fracture that could easily become a chasm. I decided I needed to get to the Hangzhou headquarters as soon as possible to meet the team in China. If the Alibaba iceberg began to calve off Hong Kong, I didn't want to drift off to sea.

Later that week I received a fax that offered me the welcome excuse to travel to Hangzhou. It was an inquiry from Justin Doebele, a journalist for *Forbes* who had just been assigned a story about Alibaba for an edition of the magazine set to focus on B2B websites. He wanted to travel to the company's head-quarters to meet Jack and the other founders and get a sense of the company. So I invited him to travel with me to the mainland, where the company had organized a retreat for the Hangzhou-based staff. I prayed the situation on the mainland would be much less dysfunctional than what I'd seen in Hong Kong so far.

ALIBABA'S CAVE

BRIAN WONG AND I PACED AROUND THE ARRIVAL
area of the Shanghai airport, killing time as we waited for Justin Doebele's plane to arrive.

"Yo, Dawg, you're lucky you joined the company when you did," Brian said. "At least the Hangzhou team finally moved into a new office last month. I spent the whole winter working in the Alibaba apartment. It was so cold we had to wear gloves while we worked."

In the short time we'd worked together Brian and I had already developed a brotherly rivalry. Hence his ribbing about having been at the company back in the "tough times," before life at Alibaba had become more comfortable.

"Yeah, it must have been a lot tougher than living with your parents in Palo Alto," I jabbed back. "You must have been jonesin' all winter for a Starbucks frappuccino." Brian chuckled.

We picked up Justin and began the two-hour drive to Nanbei Lake, a lakeside resort area between Shanghai and Hangzhou. Justin, who is tall, skinny, and slightly bookish, had just been named the Asia bureau chief for *Forbes* magazine. He was based in Singapore and had traveled to Shanghai to write about Jack Ma and Alibaba.

For me, as the company's new PR person, it was a bit of a gamble to bring the Asia bureau chief of a major business magazine along on my first trip to the Alibaba headquarters, as I had no idea what the company was actually like. It was like bringing a restaurant customer into the kitchen. And it didn't help that, because of a shortage of rooms, Justin had been assigned to share one of the resort's cabins with me, a notorious snorer. But I figured that, for a start-up company, any publicity was good publicity, and it was better to err on the side of openness.

We arrived at Nanbei Lake and found Alibaba staff members, about 100 young men and women, excitedly buzzing between the resort's small cabins. This was the company's first off-site retreat and an opportunity for the company to catch its breath after growing so quickly without a break. None of the expats had made the trip up from Hong Kong to attend the retreat, which I thought was strange for an all-hands outing, as I felt they were missing an important opportunity to bond with their local counterparts.

First we headed to dinner in a large dining hall with round tables. Filled with excitement and anticipation, people settled in for a long meal, laughing and chatting while course after course of local dishes was set on the table. Lazy Susans spun, and staffers picked off delicious local food with chopsticks while clinking their beer glasses at toast after toast.

I was struck by the warmth of the gathering. It didn't feel like a typical company. It felt much more like a family. Justin and I were invited to join a table full of my new colleagues. They were almost all in their mid-twenties and came from a range of

backgrounds. The sons and daughters of farmers, factory work-
ers, and businesspeople, most had joined the company in the
four weeks since I'd signed my contract.

As I chatted with the staff, I was struck by how much all
this meant for them. Several years earlier, even Chinese with
college degrees would have been assigned to jobs by the government, with little choice about their future. The options for
young people were terribly limited. The best they could hope
for was to get a job in a state-owned enterprise, with the government, or—if they really dreamed big—with a multinational
company. Compared to the opportunities available to the expat
staff in Hong Kong, few places in China allowed young people
to forge their own paths. Alibaba represented hope for them.

Thinking about all this made me feel a little guilty. Here I
was, an expat making nearly 50 times more than many of the
local colleagues who had hired me. Yet they were welcoming
me with open arms. My earlier concern about money began to
melt away as the full significance of Alibaba's mission dawned
on me. If we could make Alibaba a true success story, it could
reshape the future for this bright young team.

After dinner we were sent into a dance hall, its drabness
dressed in velvet drapes and sparkling with multicolored disco
lights. The room was at full capacity, and the walls were lined
with chairs. We sat along the perimeter facing each other. Jack
took the stage and addressed us over the strong reverb of the
karaoke machine.

"Wow, when we started Alibaba, I never imagined we would
someday have this many people. It's hard to believe how quickly
we've grown. I'm so happy with our progress so far. Alibaba has
got about 200,000 registered members and businesses joining

us from almost every country now. That's a good start, but it is really only the beginning of our dream. I know people think it is crazy, but we need to do everything we can to reach our goal of having one million Alibaba users from around the world by the end of the year."

The crowd applauded.

"We've all been working very hard these days, and so I'm really happy that we finally have our first staff outing," Jack went on. "We've now got an office in London, Hong Kong, Silicon Valley, and so many great new managers and staff from all around the world joining Alibaba every day. They couldn't all come today, but we do have a couple *laowai* [foreigners] here in attendance. So why don't we invite Porter, who is heading our company's international PR, to the stage to say a few words. Porter?"

The crowd grew silent and stared as I walked toward the stage. For Jack Ma the English teacher, interacting with Westerners was natural. But most of the staff had never worked with a foreigner, and I was pretty sure that many had never even spoken to one. So I felt a bit of pressure to set the right tone and bridge the gap.

In my less-than-perfect Chinese I reached into my limited quiver of jokes to break the ice. "I apologize, as my Chinese is not great and there may be some people here who don't understand what I'm saying. But let me reassure you, this is normal. Even I don't understand what I'm saying."

The crowd broke into laugher and applauded. Whew, I thought, ice broken. I went on.

"On behalf of all the foreigners who just joined the company, I want to say that we are really looking forward to being a part of the team. We are chasing the biggest dream of all—building a global company from China. I and the other foreigners on the team really look forward to working together with everyone."

The crowd gave a warm round of applause. Even though my Chinese wasn't perfect, I'd always found that just making the effort went a long way in building rapport. My words were well received. But in the back of my mind I couldn't help but worry a bit about the sizable gap between the expats in Hong Kong and the staff in mainland China.

Jack said a few more words and wrapped up the evening's events. "Just remember, everyone. We will win. We will make it. Because we are young. And we never ever give up."

It seemed so simple, even a bit naive. I looked around the room and wondered, Is this really the right team to stand up to the US Internet titans? Yet their optimism was somehow infectious. It made you want to believe.

The next day we drove two hours to Alibaba's new Hangzhou offices, stopping along the roadside to uproot bamboo shoots, which the staff wanted to bring back to their families for dinner that night. The office was housed in a drab building on the outskirts of Hangzhou, but inside it was popping with activity. With Justin in tow we strolled around the busy halls. It wasn't quite clear whether people knew exactly what they were doing, but they certainly seemed to be having fun.

At one end of the office we came to a solid door. Curious, we opened it, revealing a dark room of bunk beds filled with napping engineers. The stench of bad breath and dirty socks filled the air, punctuated by periodic snoring. Brian had told me that it was common for Alibaba's team to sleep on the floor at the Alibaba apartment, and it looked like this quirk of company culture had carried over. It seemed a good indicator of just how hard the team had been working.

I parked Justin outside Jack's office and went in to brief Jack before the interview. This was my first time prepping him, and I wanted to make sure he recognized the significance. "Jack, this is *Forbes* magazine. It's the oldest and one of the most influential business magazines in the US. So it's pretty important. They are doing a big story about B2B companies. And they are even considering making Alibaba the cover story."

"Oh, really?" he seemed surprised. "Sounds pretty important. What do you think I should say?"

I thought for a second about the team in Hong Kong and their request to keep Jack out of the spotlight—or at least keep him "on message." And then I looked at Jack and thought about the team that I had just seen at the retreat.

"Just be yourself, Jack—it's gotten you this far."

Justin came in. Jack jumped around from topic to topic, sharing his life story and vision for Alibaba. Rather than rambling on about boring MBA frameworks and business models, Jack spoke in metaphors: In the Internet era, he explained, "one must run as fast as a rabbit but be as patient as a turtle."

Justin ate it up. Jack sounded nothing like a CEO. But that's what made him so fascinating.

AROUND THE WORLD
WITH JACK

THE MAY SUNSHINE BROKE THROUGH THE CLOUDS,
hitting the trees in full bloom. This was Berlin at its best. Coming off a cold, dreary winter, Berliners and tourists alike lined the city's outdoor cafes and beer gardens to celebrate the arrival of spring. Soaking up the scene, I marveled at my luck in working for a Chinese company but spending a few weeks in the spring of 2000 traveling in Europe.

I strolled through the city with Jack and Abir Oreibi, the recently hired head of Alibaba's new European operations. Born in Libya, raised in Switzerland, and a former resident of Shanghai who was fluent in five languages, Abir was the perfect guide to introduce Jack and me to Europe. Jack bounced along, asking Abir questions about Berlin with a cheery curiosity. With a common interest in foreign languages and cultures, the three of us quickly bonded.

Beyond exploring Berlin, our European tour had a serious business purpose. This was our big PR assault on Europe. We had set up a three-city media tour for Jack to generate some publicity for Alibaba as a way of attracting importers and exporters in Europe to use Alibaba.com. With Barcelona, Berlin, and London on the agenda, we had high hopes that our Europe trip would generate significant awareness of the website through a series of high-level events and media interviews.

We arrived at the massive Messe Berlin convention center, greeted by Internet World 2000 banners and rows of corporate flags flapping in the wind. As we picked up our name badges, thousands of attendees and exhibitioners streamed in and out of the venue. It was just as we'd imagined it. The largest Internet conference in Europe, Internet World was the place to be. With high hopes we zipped through the conference hall to the main keynote area, where Jack was set to give his speech.

Determined to make a grand entrance, we burst through the doors to a venue packed with 500 seats. But wait—only three were filled.

Was this the right room? We rechecked the conference hall's floor plan. It was. But apparently the Alibaba revolution had not yet reached Europe.

An Internet World staff member stepped to the podium and leaned into the microphone. "Our next speaker is the founder and CEO of Alibaba.com. Please welcome to the stage Jack Ma."

The hollow sound of six hands clapping echoed through the conference hall.

Jack jumped on stage, put on a brave face, and with an impassioned spirit began his speech to the room of empty seats. His speech was just as much about his life as it was about Alibaba. And, as with the other two times I had heard him speak in public, it was highly entertaining. Jack was a great storyteller, and Abir and I stood at the back of the room laughing.

The applause was enthusiastic, even if it was from just three people. So maybe we hadn't conquered Europe. But our trip to Berlin had attracted at least three new revolutionaries.

Jack walked off the stage and said to Abir and me, "So, what did you think?"

"Great speech, Jack. We just wish there were more people here to hear it."

With a mischievous smile Jack leaned over and whispered, "Don't worry. When we come back here, this place will be totally full."

ALIBABA'S
FALLING CARPET

DESPITE OUR FAILURE IN BERLIN, OUR STOPS IN
London and Barcelona went better, and the international media were beginning to take a greater interest. In July 2000 we received a major boost when *Forbes* put Justin Doebele's story about Jack Ma on the cover of the magazine's "Best of the Web: B2B" edition. The coverage helped push Alibaba's global recognition to a new level and gave us the credibility we needed to attract businesses to the site.

At the same time Alibaba's website traffic continued to grow, as small businesses decided to try e-commerce. Each day we added thousands of new members as the website's reach extended globally. Manufacturers posted their product listings on the site. And buyers from around the world were sending inquiries to the sellers. Although the site was little more than a message board for companies to post trade leads, it offered a cost-effective new way for importers and exporters to find each other. The company wasn't generating any revenues, but the marketplace was growing along with Alibaba's reputation both inside and outside China.

But while Alibaba's growing reputation and traffic gave outsiders the impression we were on an upswing, the truth was that the organization faced a dangerous period of disarray. With Jack constantly on the road speaking at conferences and media events, and no chief operating officer to manage the company's day-to-day functioning, there was a leadership vacuum. The company had grown too quickly, and chaos was beginning to pull it apart.

Routine meetings included as many as 30 people, each shouting louder than the next to get their voices heard. Staff members were free to set their own schedule, making it impossible to coordinate decisions. It was not uncommon for new employees to arrive at the company for their first day of work only to find they had no defined responsibilities or clear reporting lines. This created awkward situations, such as when one new employee sat at a desk for a week pretending to be working, too afraid that asking who his boss was might result in the elimination of his job.

As these operations spun out of control, Alibaba's strategy was also in disarray. With growing pressure to develop a viable business model, the company launched a new initiative each day, trying to find a product idea that would generate revenues and cover the company's growing costs. We tried banner ads. Revenue-sharing partnerships. Website development for small businesses. We tried everything, but nothing stuck. It was a race for revenue. And a race we were losing.

After watching the team in Hangzhou fail to find a product that customers would pay for, the international management team in Hong Kong decided we needed to do the next best thing—build what investors were looking for. As the Internet industry's decline snowballed and Internet companies struggled to attract investors, the overwhelming consensus of the analysts at the leading investment banks was that, if you wanted to build a successful B2B marketplace, you had to build a platform that allowed buyers and sellers around the world to do end-to-end transactions. So, for example, if you were a sporting goods re-tailer in the United States, you could buy 10,000 tennis racquets from China with just the click of a button. Or, if you were an importer of kitchenware in Uzbekistan, ordering 2,000 coffee mugs from Vietnam would be as easy as ordering a book from Amazon.

In mid-2000 the heads of strategy for the Hong Kong team convinced Jack that, to create this all-encompassing platform for global trade, Alibaba would have to move its website opera-tions from Hangzhou to Silicon Valley. "It's where all the global Internet companies are located, Jack," he was told. "If we want to build an English-language website for the whole world, we have to go where the skilled employees are."

It seemed a valid argument. After all, there was no precedent for a global website to be run out of China. And, looking at his own team in Hangzhou, even Jack must have questioned its abil-ity to compete with Silicon Valley talent. So he announced to the team that he would move Alibaba's English website from China to California. "That's the decision we have to make. Maybe it's the wrong decision. But I always remember one thing: a wrong decision is better than no decision in Internet time."

Soon thereafter a group of Alibaba's core management posi-tions were relocated to the United States. John Wu, the recently hired chief technology officer who had come over from Yahoo! US, was to head the US engineering team. Within months Alibaba had hired about 30 new staff members in the US office, working out of Fremont, California. The decision was portrayed to both staff and outsiders as a sign of Alibaba's increasing globalization, but it ultimately proved to be a disaster, sending the company into a tailspin. Time, distance, and language differences made communication between teams highly inefficient. Just as the China team was waking up, the US staff was leaving the office. And before long Alibaba had grown into a two-headed monster, with each head going in a different direction. With a large advertising budget, growing staff costs to support the Silicon Valley office, and a lack of revenues to make up for it, Alibaba was running out of money. The company was in crisis. Something had to be done.

BACK TO CHINA

THE MORNING SUNLIGHT BROKE THROUGH THE
blinds, casting slices of shadow across the wall. Jetlagged and
disoriented, I looked around the unfamiliar room, trying to remember exactly where I was. From outside the bedroom door
I heard muted voices speaking in an unfamiliar dialect, and it
all came rushing back. Keen to avoid the inevitable, I pulled the
covers over my head and, for the next few hours, floated in and
out of sleep.

But nothing could stop the clock. The house was coming to
life. First it was the banging of shower doors. Then the clanging
of pots and pans. When the TV came on, blaring the Chinese
news, I knew I could hide no longer. The team would be waiting. I dreaded seeing them.

I pulled on my pants, tossed on a shirt, and stumbled downstairs. In the living room I found a scattered mess of used chopsticks, dirty dishes, and crumpled pillows and blankets. Against
one wall were a few flimsy card tables holding desktop computers. Next to them were half-eaten bowls of instant noodles that
must have been there for days, judging by the crusty masses

hardening at the bottom of the bowls. The curtains were closed, adding to the stuffiness of a room dominated by a stale cloud of morning breath.

Had I been in China, the scene would have been all too familiar. But I wasn't in China. I was in Fremont, California. And this was the Alibaba House.

Just three days earlier I had been sitting at my desk in Hong Kong and looking forward to a weekend boat cruise. But then Joe Tsai called. We were cutting the staff for our newly opened Silicon Valley office. He wanted me to go with Jack to California to deliver the message. And, oh yeah, I'd be staying at the Alibaba House.

The Alibaba House, it turned out, was the American version of the Alibaba apartment in which the company was founded. Within the company the Alibaba apartment was already as legendary as Apple's garage or Yahoo!'s trailer. It had also become a symbol of Alibaba's frugal, waste-no-renminbi culture. The same culture had apparently been applied to the United States, and to save hotel costs the company had rented a house in the middle of the Fremont suburbs to accommodate team members sent over from Hangzhou. The company had rented the house in the spring of 2000, when our US expansion seemed boundless. Now, just six months later, and with many of the employees sent from China already recalled back to the China headquarters, the Alibaba House seemed haunted by their ghosts.

I looked around, wondering what my Kellogg classmates would think if they could see me in a group house with my colleagues; I was living like a foreigner in my own country. Surely my classmates were brunching on lobster in a five-star Silicon

Valley hotel somewhere nearby. Meanwhile I was rummaging through the refrigerator for any food with a readable label.

Perched in front of the television set were two Chinese men wielding chopsticks and slurping bowls of noodles, catching up on the latest Chinese news. They seemed surprised to see me walk down the stairs. Apparently nobody had told them that they would have an additional housemate for the week. The awkwardness was heightened when I greeted them in English, to which they responded with puzzled looks. When I slid into Mandarin, it put them at ease.

"Hi, I'm Porter. I'm in charge of our international PR."

"Oh, hi, we're engineers," one said. "We've been working on moving the English site to the US."

They had been in the United States only a few weeks and were still excited about being there. Living and working in the world's Internet epicenter was a dream few engineers in China would ever realize. The two Alibaba engineers told me that at one point the house had been crammed full of engineers from Hangzhou. During the last few weeks the numbers had shrunk, as engineers were pulled back to China. When they asked me what I was doing in the United States, I didn't know what to say. How was I supposed to tell them that I was there to lay off their colleagues?

The doorbell saved me for the moment. It was Tony Yiu, an Alibaba founder who had arrived to drive me to the office. "You ready?" he asked. Not really, I thought, but let's go anyway.

Stepping through the front door of the house was like leaving China and entering America. The crisp color of freshly cut lawns, fluorescent street signs, and a cloudless blue sky reminded me I was back in California. As we drove through the suburbs,

I wondered how anything new was ever invented in Silicon Valley. It was so polished, so mature, with every possible convenience. Even the Jamba Juice outlets were perfectly positioned so one never had to go a stretch without a berry boost of some kind. Compared to China, which felt like one large unfinished construction site, Silicon Valley seemed finished—like everything that needed doing had been done. I wondered if one day everyone would just quit work and Rollerblade into retirement.

We drove past a few remaining dot-com billboards, turned into a small office park, and pulled up to a glossy one-story office building surrounded by a parking lot. "We're here," Tony said.

We walked into the office, and Tony took me around to meet the staff. There was a mix of Westerners, Chinese Americans, and Chinese nationals, most of whom had studied and lived in the United States for several years. Ordinarily meeting new staff members would be a happy affair, but I felt somewhat like the grim reaper. I wore a strained smile, knowing that in a few minutes I'd be laying off many of them.

I was taken to an office where Jack was reading his email. He was visibly concerned about the meeting ahead.

"I don't know what to say today," he said. "This whole time we've been growing, I've only been hiring people. This is the first time we've ever had to fire people. How do we do this?"

I felt bad for Jack. Although many of the foreign staff members didn't view him as a credible manager, I knew that only his good intentions and optimism had brought us this far. For a Chinese company, opening a Silicon Valley office was a huge source of pride. For the last several months we'd been traveling around China boasting about our growing US staff, holding it up as a sign of Alibaba's global importance.

After discussing the best way to handle it, we called the employees into a large meeting room. There was a tangible pall, as people sensed bad news was coming. Some were meeting Jack for the first time, and I hoped that the session would not become hostile.

After the seats around the table filled up, another row of colleagues formed behind them, filling the room to the walls. Once everyone was settled, we closed the door and Jack began to speak.

"I want everyone to know how much we appreciate how hard everyone is working. But I'm afraid that I'm here with some bad news. We are going to have to cut some of our staff."

Around the room eyes dropped. Jack continued:

"A few months ago we thought it would be best to move our operations to Silicon Valley. Everyone thought that if you are going to run an English-language website, this is where you have to be. The engineers are here, the English speakers are here, and the Internet people are all here. So it really seemed like the right decision at the time.

"But since we did that, it seems we created more problems in the company than ever before. Everyone here has been working so hard on different projects, but the communication is very difficult between here and our Hangzhou office. When you guys come into the office, it is the end of the day in Hangzhou. When we come into the office, you are all leaving. It seems it's been impossible to communicate, and I know you've all been frustrated when projects were started and then canceled.

"For all of us Alibaba is a dream. Everyone here has worked so hard and really believes in this dream. We want to make this a company that lasts 80 years. But if we want to make this dream happen, we have to be realistic. Right now it doesn't make sense for us to have a big center in Silicon Valley. If we want to make the company grow again someday, we are going to have to cut back today.

"I feel really bad and sorry, for you and your families. At the end of the day the mistakes we made are my responsibility. So I'm very sorry for this. I hope that someday, when the company is healthy, we can grow again and give you another chance to join Alibaba."

It was an emotional speech and, as was usual for Jack, straight from his heart. I looked around the room, and the hostility I feared had not materialized. People seemed to respect Jack's candor and were resigned to the decision he had made. The only remaining question was who would be cut, and my job was to tell them.

We were laying off about half the staff, and that sent a chill through the office. Although I didn't know the staff personally, my stomach churned each time I sat down with one of the unlucky. The company offered laid-off staff members three months of salary and allowed them to keep some of their stock options. To my surprise many were not as concerned about losing their jobs as they were sad to be leaving Alibaba. Even some of the Western staff in the office, many of whom had no personal connection to China, seemed attached to the company and its mission.

Back at the Alibaba House, I collapsed on the couch, glad to have a difficult day behind me. The company's future was still uncertain, but at least we were taking the painful steps necessary to survive. It was also clear that if any company could subsist on a tiny budget, we could do it. After all, Alibaba's founders had paid themselves a salary of only RMB 500 ($60) per month in the company's early days. Compared to the employees of our global competitors, we could more easily go back to living on a shoestring budget. Our "Back to China" strategy had begun, and if we had to, the team could contract all the way back to the Alibaba apartment, cutting costs along the way. Now, if only we had a revenue model, I thought to myself, we just might have a chance.

A few days later, after Jack and I returned to China, he called me. I was surprised to hear a shaky voice on the other end of the line.

"Porter, can I ask you a question?" His voice was breaking; it sounded like he might even be crying.

"Sure, Jack. What's wrong?"

"Am I a bad person?"

In the eight months I'd known him, I'd never seen his optimism or confidence waver.

"What do you mean?"

"I'm getting a lot of calls from staff, and they are angry with me about the layoffs. I know it was my fault that I made those decisions. And now everyone is mad at me. But do you think I'm a bad person for what I did?"

In the background I could hear Jack sniffling. I felt sad for him. Given all of the chaos and disorganization in the company, I had seen this day coming. But rather than being angry at our CEO for letting the company fall into such disarray, I was sympathetic. In my mind Jack was still just an English teacher who had reached for the stars. It was hard to blame him for overreaching.

"Jack, you did what you had to do. The company wouldn't survive if you didn't make those decisions."

"Yeah, I guess you're right. But I just feel like I let everyone down."

We spoke for a few more minutes and then hung up. I felt even more unsettled than I had on the morning of the layoffs. If Jack lost his confidence, who would be left to encourage us?

LAST MAN STANDING

NOT LONG AFTER JACK AND I RETURNED FROM THE
United States, Joe pulled me into his office. "Porter, I need you
to prepare an Alibaba organizational chart," he explained.
"We're bringing in another candidate for chief operating officer,
Savio Kwan, and I'd like you to bring the org chart along when
you interview him so that he can have a better understanding of
Alibaba's company structure."

In any other company this would have been a simple and
straightforward task, but in the case of Alibaba it was daunting.
Alibaba was almost two years old and had never had an organizational chart. I didn't particularly relish the task of trying to
make sense out of the amorphous blob that was our structure.

Internal chaos was the price we were paying even as Jack
boasted publicly, "Alibaba doesn't plan." New departments
formed and disbanded so quickly that nobody had a good sense
of who was doing what and who was in charge. Day-to-day
decisions were difficult to make without having Jack weigh in.
Important personnel decisions, such as the hiring and firing of
new staff, were made without any clear procedures, resulting in

anger and resentment among staff members who felt they were being treated unfairly. The organizational chart would be a pain in the ass to put together, but the prospect of having an adult in the room, in the form of a COO, was enough to motivate me.

As I set out to draft the organizational chart, I contacted the managers I thought were in charge of the various departments that had popped up in the previous six months, as the company swelled from 40 to several hundred employees. Not surprisingly my guesses were not always correct. Like a pinball I was bounced around to various colleagues who clearly didn't know what departments existed or who, in fact, was in charge. After hammering out the best chart I could, I realized that not everyone in the company had been accounted for. Partly to cover my bases, and partly as an ironic joke to myself, I placed an asterisk next to the chart and, at the bottom of the page, wrote:

If you do not see yourself on this organizational chart, it does not mean that you are not employed by Alibaba.

By the time I sat down with Savio, he seemed just as confused as I was—in fact, he was frazzled by the whole Alibaba interview process. "So who have you met so far?" I asked.

"I've had about eight meetings so far with the company founders, and it really seems like there's a lot of confusion."

A 25-year management veteran, with 15 of those years spent at General Electric, he was no doubt used to a more structured organization. While interviewing at Alibaba, he'd been tossed from manager to manager with no proper introductions.

"I can't understand why all these people are interviewing me. It's pretty unorthodox for a COO to be interviewed by his potential subordinates. And no one seems to have clear agreement on what the company's strategy or priorities are."

I was afraid that we'd already scared Savio away. Seeking to bring some calm to the situation, I pulled out a folder with the Alibaba organizational chart I'd created, along with a few articles and background material about Alibaba that gave as close to a comprehensive introduction to the company as was possible at the time. He took a deep breath and seemed to feel a bit more at ease.

"Eight meetings in, this is the first time anyone has given me any kind of overview of Alibaba," he said. I could only imagine what had been discussed in his earlier meetings.

Savio settled in and told me a little bit about himself. He had been born and raised in Hong Kong, then had studied in London, and ultimately found his way back to China, helping lead GE's medical equipment business there in the 1980s and '90s. He had been working in China at a time when few people from Hong Kong were willing to do so, and that had given him a front-row seat for China's transition from a planned economy to a market economy. It gave me some comfort to know that he had worked in China before doing so became a trend and would probably be accustomed to a rough-and-tumble environment.

Savio was not the first person whom I'd interviewed for the position, and my first impression of him was that he wasn't the best candidate. He had a warm and jovial spirit that told me he might fit in, and the graying hair that signaled experience, but I worried that he lacked the industry expertise and decisiveness necessary to bring order to Alibaba's chaos. I preferred the first candidate I'd met, a strong, bold—even brash—China country manager from a large multinational tech company who seemed like he'd bring real backbone to the company. Savio seemed almost too nice. I shared my thoughts with Joe Tsai.

"So you liked the other guy?" Joe responded. "Well, I don't think we're going to be able to get him. He's in a pretty high-level position at his current company, and in this market it would be hard to convince him to join a little start-up like Alibaba."

In January 2001 we announced that Savio was our new COO. And a few weeks after that Savio surprised me with his decisiveness by cutting the majority of the remaining international staff at the company. First he cut Hong Kong, keeping only a few financial and administrative staffers. And then he cut what was left of the US office, save for a couple technical experts. The suddenness was a shock, which left me with a strange loneliness that even the staff members with whom I'd had disagreements were now gone. With the exception of Abir Oreibi in Europe and a few other international staffers, I now found myself the lone survivor in the group hired about the same time I was.

As painful as it was, the layoffs were crucial to stop Alibaba's financial bleeding. Jack should have recognized this earlier, but doing it took an outsider who did not have personal relationships with the staff. In the wake of the layoffs I arrived at work to see rows upon rows of empty desks where my colleagues used to sit.

In severing the international staff, the company had made an attempt to be fair. Employees were offered a choice of three months' salary or one month of salary plus two years' worth of their unearned stock options. Disgruntled and with little faith in the company's prospects, many of the laid-off managers chose the full three-month salary offer, not wanting to be left holding worthless stock certificates for a company that appeared to be headed toward bankruptcy.

Savio's next step was a more symbolic one—clearing out the bunk beds from Alibaba's main Hangzhou office. "This is unsustainable," he contended. "If people are working around the clock like this, they will burn out. We have to allow people to spend time with their families and have a life outside of Alibaba, or they won't last long in the company." On the one hand I got his point. But on the other hand, I worried that not only was he cutting staff, he was cutting back the hours that existing staff were working. Might he be bringing a big-company working culture to Alibaba without any of the actual business to justify it?

With his quick, bold cuts in staff, Savio had defied my initial impression of him as lacking conviction. But cutting costs was one thing. Building a business was another. And Savio's next moves failed to impress me. Rather than taking the company by the reins, defining its strategy, and moving forward with a bold execution plan, Savio decided to focus senior management on a lengthy process of defining the company's mission, vision, and values.

Hadn't we been talking about these things for more than a year already? I thought to myself. If there was one thing that Alibaba had been big on, it was talking about dreams and values. Our problem, it seemed to me, was that we had a lot of lofty talk and not enough tangible results. With Alibaba's money running out, shouldn't we be doing more than writing down typical corporate-speak on PowerPoint presentations?

After a couple months on the job, Savio made a trip to the Shanghai office, where I'd been working, to present what Jack and the Alibaba cofounders had been working on. Savio led us through the slide presentation:

> We've made a lot of organizational changes lately as we've cut back staff and moved our operations to China, as you know, but we have to make clear to everyone that we have only two options from here: grow or die. We all believe in this business for the long term, and we have one great advantage over all of our foreign competitors, which is that we can keep our costs much lower in China. So as our competitors fall each day, we just have to achieve one thing—to be the last man standing.
>
> In the last few months I've been meeting with Jack and the company founders, and we've hammered out the company's mission, vision, and values. I'm here to present them to you today:
>
> First, Alibaba's mission: To make doing business easy.
>
> Next, Alibaba's vision: To be a partner to all business people.
>
> Finally, Alibaba's nine values: Passion, innovation, teach and learn, openness, simplicity, teamwork, focus, quality, customer first.

Savio stood back from the projection screen with a dramatic pause to give us all a chance to soak it in. As I sat in the silence, I couldn't help but be disappointed.

That's it? I thought. *Three months in and this is all we've come up with? A few touchy-feely PowerPoint slides about mission, vision, and values?*

Savio went on:

These are the core values that everyone will be evaluated on. From now on, everyone will have a quarterly review and score-card. 50 percent of your points will be based on your performance in reaching goals. The other 50 percent of your points will be based on how well you adhered to Alibaba's core values.

I was starting to catch on. This was actually going to be a part of a process.

Savio continued:

And with these values, we will have a new system for hiring, evaluating, promoting, and firing staff. From now on each personnel decision will be made according to "one over one plus HR." So for each employee's review, four people will be present. The employee. The employee's manager. The employee's manager's manager. And a representative from HR. This is going to ensure that our personnel decisions are clear and consistent across the company.

This type of review system was new to me but it seemed to make sense. As Savio introduced these systems he'd brought with him from GE, I could see that Alibaba's organization and procedures were beginning to take shape.

"We're also initiating something new—we'll have two tracks for people to advance within the company," Savio said. "There will be a management track for people who would like to move up in the organization as managers. And a 'specialist track' for specialists, so that they can also advance in the company."

This was an idea that had never occurred to me, but once Savio explained it, it made perfect sense. The natural tendency for a company is to promote a high-performing specialist, such as an engineer or graphic designer, to the position of manager. Most employees would accept this because they want to see their salary and recognition increase. But not every skilled specialist makes a great manager. Alibaba had made this mistake several times and in the process lost a great specialist while gaining a terrible manager. It usually didn't take long for the role mismatch to become so uncomfortable that the manager left the company or was forced out.

Savio's next step was to announce training tracks for the team. Entry-level employees, such a sales staff, would be put through a training program tailored to their specific functional skill in the company. Managers would participate in separate training tracks focused on developing their management skills. In addition each new employee would receive at least a week of orientation to the company. At the core of these training tracks were Alibaba's mission, vision, and values.

As Savio wrapped up, I was still slightly skeptical but I decided to keep an open mind and give Savio and his plan a chance. He did have 25 years of business experience, after all. Maybe there was more to Savio's approach than met the eye. Plus, Savio seemed to appreciate the urgency of rescuing Alibaba's deteriorating balance sheet and was beginning to focus management's attention on coming up with a strategy to actually make money.

In the next few months we batted around ideas about how the company could generate revenue. Unable to make money on our own website, we discussed the idea of selling e-commerce solutions to local governments in China, with the idea that they might build "Alibabies" that local businesses could use as platforms for posting their products online. After knocking on a few government doors with this idea, and quickly realizing that local government officials would demand bribes and kickbacks from us in exchange for purchasing an Alibaby, we dropped it. Following the Alibaby strategy might keep us out of bankruptcy, but it might also put us in jail.

As we struggled to find a way to make money, we noticed an interesting trend. At just about the time that sellers on Alibaba.com were beginning to make deals with overseas buyers they'd met on the website, their product listings on Alibaba.com were being crowded out by the increasing number of competitors who were signing up for Alibaba. So, for example, the first electric scooter manufacturer on Alibaba received all the inquiries from interested buyers around the world and, with no competition, had little incentive to pay Alibaba for the free service he was receiving. But over time he was increasingly crowded out by a growing number of scooter sellers who were joining the site and posting their products online. Sellers began to ask us for the opportunity to pay us for a sponsored listing of their products so that they could appear above Alibaba's organic search results. It appeared that, after giving Alibaba's services away for free for two years, we had finally reached the critical point at which customers were willing to pay.

In spring of 2001 our budding sales team decided to focus its efforts on a product we'd test-launched called China Supplier. For roughly $2,000 an exporter in China got a nicer-looking company profile, could post more product listings than a standard member, and received priority listing for the exporter's products in Alibaba's search results. For a typical manufacturer $2,000 was a bargain compared to the costs of advertising in an expensive trade publication or traveling to the United States or Europe to attend an industry trade show to display products. While a magazine advertisement might be obsolete after one month, and a trade show would last only a week, the Internet offered these sellers an opportunity to run their online trade show on Alibaba 24 hours a day, seven days a week.

This was good news, but the lack of trust in the anonymous Wild West of the Internet still posed a difficult challenge for buyers and sellers, especially when compared to trade shows, which offered the chance to meet business partners face to face. That customers were willing to pay Alibaba for a premium listing offered a bit of confidence in their solidity to prospective buyers overseas. But it still didn't answer two key questions: Is the seller I'm communicating with a legally registered business, and does the person I'm communicating with actually work for the company?

We soon realized that it wasn't enough for sellers to have a paid listing on Alibaba. Buyers needed to have some assurance that the person they were dealing with was legitimate. So we launched a service called TrustPass. The only way to be certified with TrustPass was for a company to go through a third-party authentication-and-verification process that demonstrated that in fact it was a legal business and the person was authorized to represent the company in trade dealings.

The launch of TrustPass marked a key breakthrough for Alibaba. With it we had finally recognized that the main inhibitor of online transactions was the issue of trust. With a critical mass of buyers and sellers around the world, we had plenty of members. If we could solve the trust issue, we could crack the code of e-commerce. So we required each China Supplier to also have TrustPass verification. And this combination gave us a perfect excuse to begin to charge our customers. It made China Supplier customers, who paid for that status, appear more trustworthy. It made those members still clinging to their free accounts seem *less* trustworthy. After all, if they had such a good business, why weren't they willing to pay up a little to prove it?

With China Supplier we finally had a product that seemed feasible. But we quickly realized that selling the product on a mass scale to our members couldn't be done over the phone or the Internet. We needed to move our customers from simply testing the e-commerce waters to diving in. And to do that we'd need to meet with our customers in person.

Like a team of Pied Pipers playing the intoxicating tune of e-commerce, we spent the second half of 2001 on a national road show, inviting our customers to member gatherings up and down China's east coast, where the majority of the country's manufacturers, exporters, and trading companies were located. In city after city we opened new offices and organized launch events for our members under the theme of "Give e-commerce back to the business people." The message was one of empowerment—that the magic of the Internet allowed small businesses to compete with the largest multinationals. The message had strong appeal in a country where entrepreneurs valued their independence and believed that "it is better to be the head of a chicken than the tail of a phoenix."

The formula for each of our member events was simple. Jack's growing celebrity status helped us draw attendees. Jack would first give a talk about the future of e-commerce and how he thought small businesses could benefit from it. I was rolled out next to talk about Alibaba's overseas activities, somewhat like a talking monkey for local business people curious to see a foreigner speaking Chinese. Although the freak show got their attention, having a foreigner rather than a local present Alibaba's growing overseas reputation carried more weight to an audience that might otherwise have been skeptical of Alibaba's claims to have a strong reputation with buyers overseas. After Jack and I spoke, members of the newly hired local sales teams would take the stage to introduce the specific products and services that our new China Supplier status offered.

One by one the sales started to roll in as we traveled from city to city. With each stop I began to learn more about the unique characteristics of each city. Yongkang was known for its many electric scooter manufacturers. Ningbo, for its disposable lighters. Jinhua, for its prosciutto-like ham. Each city had its cluster of manufacturers with distinct specialties.

No trip was complete without a local team dinner at a small roadside restaurant to celebrate the establishment of each new office. My tour turned out to be a chance to try all the local delicacies. Turtle shell soup, raw crab soaked in alcohol, bamboo shoots, fruits I'd never heard of before.

What struck me most was the energy and enthusiasm of the young sales team recruits, even though they were tasked with selling Internet services at a time when most people in China had given up on e-commerce. We were in the depths of the Internet winter, so our team was not made up of recent graduates from top universities such as Beijing University or Fudan—they had far too many other well-paid options at multinationals. Instead Alibaba was attracting sales team members who'd grown up in small townships and rural areas, the sons and daughters of farmers and laborers. The pay was low and conditions harsh, but Alibaba was a small step up for them and their families—a source of hope.

We'd often visit the new offices after our customer events. The budget for each office was so low that they were often located in drab apartments in dreary, run-down buildings. The staff often slept and worked out of the tiny apartments, furnished with little more than metal frame beds on concrete floors, with fluorescent lightbulbs creating an eerie glow that bounced off the stark white walls. But no one complained about the conditions, because we all had a shared sense of ownership of the company and its potential rewards. Nearly everyone in the company had stock options; there was a spirit of shared sacrifice for the greater good of the company. Every penny saved would help Alibaba survive and grow to the benefit of all employees.

As our road show gained momentum, our presentations became more sophisticated. In a span of a few months, our events grew from tens of customers in two-star hotel conference rooms to hundreds of customers in five-star hotels. With each road show the local media reported on the growing movement that Alibaba was creating. One by one we were convincing China's business people to move online.

But despite the growing sales numbers, we still were burning through cash and not generating enough revenue to cover our costs. At the beginning of 2001, a few months after Todd Daum voluntarily left Alibaba, I had been assigned to take over his role of vice president of international marketing. My first move was to cut our advertising budget to zero. One look at Alibaba's website traffic had shown me that even without advertising support, our website had natural viral growth. So, much to the marketing team's dismay, I told them that we had changed our strategy to "zero budget marketing" and would rely solely on word of mouth and public relations to take advantage of free media coverage. Any marketing plan would have to involve no budget.

The good news was that cutting our marketing budget to zero seemed to have little impact on our website's growth—we were still growing organically through word of mouth. But the bad news was that it made our marketing team a bit obsolete. With the advertising budget eliminated, we began to focus on PR to gain free publicity. But with the web industry in a deep freeze, the media lost all interest in Internet companies. Toward the end of 2001, Jack pulled me aside for a conversation.

"Porter, I want to let you know about a decision that all of the senior managers in the company made together. Me, Joe, John, Savio—we all decided to cut our own salaries in half."

Jack had a smile on his face but also a serious look.

"So I want to let you know that you are now the highest-paid employee in the company. No one has complained about it. But I just wanted to let you know that."

I gulped as Jack walked away. I was now being paid even more than the CEO. Many of the founders of the company were living at a level that most Americans would have viewed as poverty. Not to mention that I had just visited sales offices where my own colleagues were crammed into spartan quarters, scrimping by on instant noodles and making only a few hundred dollars a month. It just didn't feel right to be paid so much more than my colleagues when the company was still not even profitable.

And of course I realized that Jack's words were a friendly hint that my salary was unsustainable. Shortly after my conversation with Jack, at my next quarterly review with Savio, we started talking about my future role at Alibaba. "Jack told me that I was the highest-paid person in the company, but I realize there's not so much of a role for marketing and PR right now," I said.

"Well, for marketing and PR, there's not as much work as before," Savio responded. "One idea we had was for you to move to the Hangzhou headquarters, where you could head operations of the international website. But it's hard to think of what you could do based in Shanghai."

I mulled it over. Hangzhou was a beautiful city that I loved to visit. But in the previous year I had already moved from Beijing to Hong Kong and then from Hong Kong to Shanghai. I wasn't quite ready for another move even further inland to a city with a tiny expat community. Plus, I had one unrelenting dream of my own that I had not yet fulfilled—to travel around the world for a year.

"I've always had this dream to travel around the world," I said. "It's something I've been wanting to do since I was a kid. Why don't I take time off, and once I've finished that, we can check back in to see if there is a greater role for me?"

Savio seemed happy with the solution. It would save the company a large lump of money and would still give us the option of my coming back. He generously offered me the same severance options he'd offered the others who'd been laid off. When I told him I'd take the three months of salary and leave the stock options on the table, he stood up from his chair and said, "Wait here for a second—I just want to check with Jack on something," before walking out of the office.

He came back with a smile on his face and surprised me, saying, "I checked with Jack, and we'd like to let you keep all of your stock options, with the hope you'll come back to the company."

It was a nice goodwill gesture but one I didn't pay much attention to. I assumed that Alibaba would at most be a $10 million company, making my options worthless, well below their strike price. To be polite I smiled and thanked him, although my hopes of becoming an Alibaba millionaire had long since been dashed. "Thanks, but don't worry about that," I said somewhat dismissively. "I hadn't even thought about the stock options."

"No, really, we'd like you to keep them. And we hope you'll come back."

I rode the train back to Shanghai, staring out the window at the rice fields, waterways, and small gray factories that dotted the countryside. I was excited to finally have the chance to realize my dream of traveling around the world. But a melancholy set in as I realized I was leaving the Alibaba dream behind. And a part of me felt I was abandoning my colleagues at a time when they needed my support. I couldn't help but wonder, after my travels were done, would Alibaba still be around?

LOCK UP

AS WE ENTERED 2003, THE YEAR OF THE SHEEP didn't come in quietly. Colorful fireworks lit up the Hangzhou skies, while the constant rat-a-tat-tat of exploding firecrackers echoed throughout my apartment complex. With my round-the-world dream finally fulfilled, I was focused and determined to dive back into Alibaba with a renewed sense of commitment. I'd enjoyed my travels and seen the world but was looking forward to enjoying the camaraderie of a start-up again. As opposed to when I first joined Alibaba, money was not a significant motivation the second time around and I agreed to come back for half my previous salary. Working as one of only two Westerners in a Chinese environment would be a great way to improve my Chinese-language skills, I figured.

After the celebrations in the street had died down, Alibaba organized an all-company gathering at a hotel to kick off the new year. I was curious to see how Alibaba had changed since I'd left. When I arrived at the hotel, I was pleasantly surprised to hear cheers and the thumping of dance music emanating from the conference room and to see so many new faces streaming in.

The mood was 180 degrees from where it had been a year earlier. Just a few months before, the company had finally become profitable, and tonight was the night to celebrate.

Joining in the frenzy was Savio Kwan, cheering and chanting along with the staff, most of whom were 20 years his junior. Seeing the turnaround in company morale and performance, it was immediately clear how wrong I'd been in my first impressions of Savio's management style. I'd come full circle to appreciate that Savio was exactly the COO that Alibaba had needed. Savio hadn't provided a rigid backbone for the company. Instead, he had provided an exoskeleton—outer constraints that helped keep the company from growing out of control. His emphasis on codifying Alibaba's values proved to be the critical formula that allowed the company to grow larger while maintaining its start-up spirit and strong team culture. It was exactly what our young company needed to allow new leaders to emerge from the pack.

One such leader was Liqi, my new boss and the head of international operations. With the room full and the music pumping, Liqi jumped on stage, grabbed a microphone, and invited everyone to start dancing. We swarmed the stage, jumping up and down as balloons bounced and flags waved, chanting and cheering in the euphoria of knowing that Alibaba was finally on the upswing. After a cold, dark Internet winter, spring had arrived.

On my first day back in the office, I sat down with Liqi to discuss the year's strategy. He was short, pudgy, and wore huge black-rimmed glasses, which made him look a bit like a Chinese member of Run-DMC. He had a deep, raspy voice and a sharp, slightly dirty, sense of humor that kept the staff doubled over during meetings. But behind all that, Liqi was incredibly tough. In contrast to Jack's open, consensus-building style, Liqi's focused on action and results, the only things that mattered to him. Style points meant nothing.

Whereas Jack's life experiences had made him equally comfortable among Chinese and foreigners, Liqi's relationship with foreigners was complicated. Like a lot of Chinese, he seemed to simultaneously admire and resent Americans. Of course some of the resentment was justified. He once described to me how he'd gone to a top Guangzhou university in the 1980s but wasn't allowed to enter the five-star Garden Hotel there because he was a local Chinese. Foreigners, on the other hand, could wander in and out of the hotel freely—policy at the time when China was just opening up and it was assumed local Chinese didn't have the means to stay at the hotel themselves. Liqi could read and understand English well but was uncomfortable speaking it, so all our meetings were held in Chinese. It was a huge help to my language skills but made it much more difficult to argue my case in strategy discussions.

Nevertheless I admired Liqi. He had joined up with Jack in the days of China Pages, and Liqi had the true spirit of an entrepreneur. And with firmness and decisiveness, Liqi had built up Alibaba's national sales force, a key factor in its reaching profitability. A street-smart, no-nonsense manager, he was a perfect counterweight to Jack. If Jack was a budding Bill Gates, Liqi was his Steve Ballmer. Given my own tendency to be a bit too laidback, I realized that working for someone like Liqi would be good for me.

"Porter, we haven't worked together before, so we will have to take time to get used to each other's style," Liqi said directly that first day. "One thing I can say is that I care about results. You are going to be judged based on the numbers you deliver. And there's one main thing you're going to be focused on— getting buyers to Alibaba. We've done a great job of signing up China Suppliers for the last year, but now we need to feed them. We finally have enough money to end our zero budget marketing strategy. But we need a cost-effective way to attract buyers from around the world to support our sales. Until now we haven't had a breakthrough. And you need to find that breakthrough."

"Yes, I understand. Buyer, buyer, buyer," I said, sounding as confident as I could. But behind my facade of confidence I was nervous. Where was I going to find a breakthrough?

As we discussed the year ahead, we looked at the calendar. "In April the Canton Fair is going on in Guangzhou," Liqi added. "There are going to be buyers from all around the world there. Our sales team is going to have a huge booth there to meet with and sell to Chinese suppliers. So make sure to leave room on your calendar for that."

I welcomed the prospect of heading to the China Import and Export Fair, also called the Canton Fair, in a couple months. As an event it could be grueling, involving long hours standing up at booths and fighting through massive crowds. But at least it would allow me to go out and network with Alibaba's international buyers, speak English, and have some contact with the outside world. As much as I liked Hangzhou, I needed to come up for air from time to time.

Right around this time I began to read some unsettling reports in Western media about a mysterious new illness that was sending people in Guangzhou to the hospital. At first it seemed to be just a strange flu that affected only a handful of people. But before long the illness had a name—SARS—and a death count.

As the illness spread from Guangzhou to densely populated Hong Kong, panic set in. The Western news programs showed scenes of hospitals, ambulances, and people wearing face masks in the hope of protecting themselves. But the Chinese media covered up the story, afraid that reporting on it might create panic in China and hurt the economy. "There's nothing to worry about" was the message from the Chinese government.

As I read about the growing epidemic, I grew concerned for my own safety and the safety of our team if we continued with our plan to attend the Canton Fair. Heading to the epicenter of the SARS outbreak with the goal of shaking hands with thousands of strangers from all over the world seemed like just about the worst possible move at the moment. I wrote a strongly worded email to Liqi and Savio, stressing that we should reconsider our plan to attend the fair in light of the health risks to our team. Liqi's response did not encourage me:

"The government is saying that it's OK, so it's OK. I'm sure if there was a risk, they would cancel the Canton Fair and let people know it wasn't safe to come to Guangzhou. Look, Porter, I'm going and other senior managers are going too. If we don't go, it's like we are sending in the rank-and-file troops but not sending our generals. We all need to go in order to show support for our team."

It made sense. If we were still going to participate, we couldn't exactly stay back in Hangzhou while sending the entry-level staff. But I was disappointed with the decision. Sure, the

Canton Fair was our most important sales event, and canceling our booth would have cost us money. But in this case it seemed a dangerous call. Still, I couldn't blame Liqi—the national media were telling everyone in China that there was no need for widespread concern.

A few weeks later I was in Guangzhou helping run the Alibaba booth at the Canton Fair and shaking hands with buyers from Nigeria, Iran, Uzbekistan, the United States, and Latin America. If global trade was an engine of the global economy, these guys were the mechanics working under the hood. With sleeves rolled up and dirt on their hands, they lived in a world where every penny spent cut into their profit margin, and they had to constantly muscle their suppliers to squeeze out the best quality, at the best cost, and in the shortest amount of time. Battle weary from years of tough travel and negotiations, they were a far cry from the pampered investment bankers and management consultants I had gone to business school with.

That year's Canton Fair was strikingly different from those of the past. Ordinarily it's a lively hive of activity, with thousands of buyers and sellers shaking hands and sealing deals. But that year only one side of the equation had shown up—Chinese sellers. International buyers, for the most part, had stayed away. The divide between China's state-censored media and the free press of the West could not have been more apparent.

As I chatted with the few buyers who trickled in, Kitty Song from the China Supplier sales team worked alongside me, chatting with local customers. Cheery and full of energy, she managed to greet each supplier even as she fought off a cough. With so few buyers to meet, the local exporters spent more time at the Alibaba booth exploring the Internet as a potential channel to overseas buyers, who apparently did not to want to travel to China.

Although our team delivered a record number of sales following the Canton Fair, I was relieved to be safely back in Hangzhou the following week. We'd tempted fate and survived. The *gui hua* (cassia) flower was in full bloom in my neighborhood, emitting a sweet fragrance that filled the air; I had a beer in one hand and a croquet mallet in the other. I was hanging out with some Westerners I'd met in my apartment complex. A local journalist happened upon us and interviewed me about whether I was worried about SARS. (With the media blackout on the epidemic now lifted, local news teams could finally report on it.) "No, I'm not worried about it," I said. "I think it's a bit overblown. In fact, I just came back from Guangzhou and didn't experience any problems."

Back in the office, Jack stopped by my desk. He had a mischievous look on his face, as he often did when he felt he was onto a big new idea.

"How are things going now that you're back, Porter?"

"Things are good," I said. "Liqi and I are working well together."

"That's great," he replied. "Because the sales are strong and the company is doing really well. And I've made a decision that, in three years, people are going to say was the smartest decision we ever made."

My curiosity was piqued. "Really? What's that?"

"You'll just have to wait and see. It's a big one." He smiled and walked away.

The following week was the May Day holiday, otherwise known as the Golden Week, when everyone in China is given a week off from work. I took advantage of the time to get to know Hangzhou a little better. A former capital of China, its main attraction is the West Lake, the subject of countless paintings and poems. By day families and friends gather on the banks to play cards and drink Dragon Well tea, freshly plucked from terraced tea fields in neighboring villages. At night students and young graduates escape their dormitories and cramped homes to sit on the benches along the perimeter of the lake, kissing in the darkness under the willow trees.

After seven days of my Hangzhou staycation, a part of me wasn't ready to go back to work just yet. But when I suddenly got an extension, it was for all the wrong reasons.

"Porter, please don't worry about coming in to work tomorrow," the voice on the phone said. It was Monson, Alibaba's head of HR.

"What? Why is that?"

"We've discovered that one of our staff might have been infected by SARS. So you and six other people can take the day off tomorrow. We'll let you know when you need to come back in. Oh, and you'll all be *bei geli*."

"*Bei geli?* What does that mean?"

"Someone from the government is going to come by to lock your door from the outside. They just want to be safe, just in case."

I realized I was about to be quarantined.

"By the way, Monson, which one of our colleagues was diagnosed with SARS?"

"Um . . ." he paused, not quite sure whether to tell me. "Kitty. Kitty Song."

Gulp. Kitty Song? I had spent several days chatting with her, meeting the same people she did, working at her side in the trade show booth. I was worried for her sake but also my own. If she had SARS, maybe I did too.

The next morning I heard the sound of drilling outside my apartment door. And then the sounds of chains clinking. I was locked in.

I nervously contacted my parents to let them know I was under quarantine.

"Oh, the minute they let you out, please come home, Porter," my mom pleaded. "I can't bear the thought of having my only son over in China in the middle of SARS."

I tried to reassure her that I wasn't in harm's way. I felt fine, after all. But in the back of my mind I was nervous. With ten days to go before I could be declared free of symptoms, it was simply a waiting game.

I received a call from a local government official who explained how the quarantine would work. Each day a nurse dressed in protective gear would arrive to disinfect my apartment. And I'd also receive two calls to check my temperature. Although I couldn't leave my apartment, I could order any food I wanted, and the government would arrange for it to be brought over and left outside my door. *This quarantine thing might not be so bad,* I thought, and placed my first order—shrimp, broccoli, rice, and the ingredients to make a salad.

A couple of days later things took a more serious tone when Kitty's status was changed from "suspected SARS" to "confirmed SARS." With that the number of Alibaba staff members under quarantine grew from seven to 500—all employees at Hangzhou headquarters were locked in their homes, unable to come to the office. To keep the website running, 500 staffers carted their computers home and set up a virtual operation. Phones calls were rerouted to staffers' homes, and parents and siblings helped out by answering the phone.

It was a grave time for the company but worse for Kitty. Whereas I was locked in a nice apartment complex receiving special care and attention as a foreigner, Kitty had been thrown into a stark hospital room with two other SARS victims, one of whom was quickly deteriorating.

But the challenge proved to be an important one for the company, binding the team together to both keep the website running and support Kitty. During the day the team continued to work, chatting online. At night and on the weekend, team members hosted virtual karaoke contests on the company's Intranet.

Locked in my apartment, I had little to do during the day besides distract myself from health concerns by tinkering with the advertising campaign we were testing on Google's search advertising platform. I had persuaded Liqi to grant me $600 to test on Google's AdWords, and the initial results were amazing. Our biggest headache had always been that we had no cost-effective way of reaching our niche business customers in 180 countries. But advertising on Google allowed us to generate targeted traffic from such obscure key terms as "China ball-bearing supplier." From the Google ads we were suddenly generating targeted traffic from every corner of the Earth at five cents a click. My list of keyword ads quickly grew from six to 500. Could this be the breakthrough that we needed?

As Kitty slowly recovered, staff morale improved. Finally I heard the chains being removed from my door, followed by a knock. When I opened the door, I was greeted by camera flashes, police, and the local Communist Party secretary.

"You're free to come out!" they said. After seven days of confinement, I bounded outside for some blue skies and fresh air. After calling my mother to let her know I was okay, I called Jack.

"I just got out too," he said. "And they are telling me that Kitty is fine and should be out tomorrow."

It was good news all around. Not only had we survived intact, but Alibaba had embraced the challenge laid in front of it. We had managed to keep the website running seamlessly in the face of disaster. In fact, traffic had skyrocketed, as the epidemic accelerated the adoption of e-commerce in China by providing a channel for buyers and sellers to connect without the need to meet face to face. If the true measure of a company is how it weathers a crisis, we had passed with flying colors. Good thing, because we were about to face our greatest challenge yet.

WAR ON EBAY

BACK IN THE OFFICE, LIFE RETURNED TO NORMAL—
at least, normal for China. Just as SARS was burning out, a
massive heat wave strained Hangzhou's electricity grid in the
summer of 2003. Hangzhou had failed to grow its electricity
supply fast enough to keep up with the number of factories and
air conditioners added over the years, and we, along with other
companies in the area, were forced to ration electricity. On hot
days air-conditioning was not allowed, so the company had
large ice blocks stationed in plastic tubs around the office; unfortunately this had little effect. And on the hottest days Hangzhou scheduled rolling blackouts, which meant our offices were
shut down and staffers were sent home.

In the midst of all this Jack strolled into my office, once
again flashing his mischievous grin. He shut the door behind
him. "Porter, you know how I told you that we'd made a big
decision about a month ago? Well, I'm ready to tell you now.
And I'm going to need your help."

He looked around to make sure nobody was listening, and
after pausing for dramatic effect he let me in on his secret:
"We're going to war with eBay."

Wow. eBay. We'd faced down large Internet companies before, but eBay was the largest e-commerce company in the world. Not only that, but eBay had invested in a Chinese company, Eachnet, which already had a dominant market share of China's online auction market. "Okay," I said. "How do we plan to do this?"

Jack told me: "I started looking at the market and realized that, pretty soon, eBay was going to try to get aggressive with its business in China. They'd start with consumers, but over time they will start coming after Alibaba's wholesalers. Competition was inevitable. So I decided the only way we can slow them down is to launch a site to compete directly with their Chinese-language site.

"So last month, I pulled together six people in my office. I told them that I had a secret project for them. If they were interested in finding out what the job was, they would have to first resign from Alibaba and then move to work from a secret location. They couldn't tell their friends or family what they were working on. They couldn't even tell anyone at Alibaba what they were working on. I gave them a few minutes to think about it and told them that if they weren't interested, they didn't have to take the job. They could simply return to their position in Alibaba—there would be no hard feelings. A few minutes later they all came back to the room and said, 'Jack, we'll do it!'"

I smiled to myself as Jack related the story to me. Clearly it was an offer they wouldn't refuse. But rather than simply assigning them to the new project, Jack had to make the whole process dramatic and exciting, as if shaping actual events for maximum drama ten years later. It might have been a bit over the top, but it was part of what made working at Alibaba fun.

"So after they signed the agreement," Jack said, picking up his story, "I told them what the project was—to develop a consumer auction site to compete directly with Eachnet in China. And to build the site they had to go back to Alibaba's roots—my apartment in Hupan Gardens. They worked on the site while everyone was in quarantine. They launched it a few weeks ago, and it's really taking off."

He leaned over my computer and said, "Here, you can see it. It's called Taobao. It means, 'search for treasure.' Pull up Taobao.com."

I typed it in and up popped a shopping website that felt like a cross between Alibaba.com and eBay. It was pretty basic and didn't quite look like it was at the level of Eachnet. But I'd learned not to judge a work in progress, and for a website that had been up for only a few weeks, it was not bad.

"It's going really well," Jack continued. "The first users seem to love the site so far. And it's funny, there are people coming up to me at Alibaba saying, 'Jack, we should be really careful. There's a new site called Taobao that really looks and feels like Alibaba. These guys could be really good competition someday.' They have no idea `it's our own site. This is going to be huge someday."

Had it been three years earlier, I would have been a skeptic. But after seeing Jack's predictions come true in our battle against our large B2B competitors, I'd come to believe that if Jack said it was possible, he was probably right. His intuition had carried us this far. It was better to just suspend disbelief and go along with it.

"So what help do you need from me?" I asked.

"We're ready to launch Taobao. And when we do, we are going to declare war on eBay. The launch has to be a really big bomb to generate a lot of buzz in the media. I don't want this to be a war between Taobao and Eachnet. It has to be about Taobao versus eBay. This is about Alibaba's taking on Goliath."

It was trademark Jack. Just as Alibaba had finally become stable and profitable, he wanted to bet the whole company on yet another huge dream. There was no challenge too big for this guy.

"So is everyone on board with this?" I asked.

"Joe and Savio are on board. One of our senior executives told me I was crazy and threatened to leave the company if I wanted to take on eBay," Jack replied. "But after a while I convinced him as well. It looks like Masayoshi Son of Softbank will invest. He was going to invest before we got started but took too long to think about it, so we went ahead and started without him. Now, I told him, the price has gone up.

"So get ready, Porter. I know you are focused on Alibaba. com right now, but I'm going to need your help to make a big announcement soon. It's really important that we get the foreign media to start writing about this to build some momentum. We need to engage eBay in a war of words, and the only way to do that is to get them to take notice of us back in the US."

After Jack left my office I decided to head over to see the Taobao team for myself. I'd always slightly regretted not having been a part of Alibaba in its apartment days, so I decided not to miss the chance again. This could be historic, after all, and I wanted to see the secret Taobao operations with my own eyes.

I knocked on the apartment door, expecting to see a hive of activity as engineers, product developers, and website designers furiously prepared for the big launch. But it was just the opposite. It was the middle of the afternoon but the apartment was nearly empty, with the exception of two programmers sleeping on the floor next to a couple computers with black screens.

An engineer walked in from the kitchen, slurping from a bowl of noodles. "Where is everyone?" I asked.

"The power's off again in the apartment complex. They all went home to rest."

He went back into the kitchen, leaving me in the room with the two sleeping engineers. I imagined eBay's team, far away in Silicon Valley, probably working away in slick, air-conditioned headquarters with rows of servers buzzing. Meanwhile we couldn't even manage electricity. I couldn't help but wonder whether this team was going to beat the most powerful Internet company in the world.

A week later Taobao was ready for its official debut. At a packed press conference in Hangzhou, we announced that we'd be investing $12 million in the company and that we'd build a consumer marketplace customized for China. It would be free for three years. Jack argued that China needed its own model for e-commerce and that with the market still in its infancy, it was too soon to charge customers.

"Today we're not going to say how Taobao will make money. Taobao's focus right now is on how to help develop e-commerce for individuals and how to provide good services for them. I believe the market is huge. If you look at the existing consumer websites in China, most of them just copy the American model," Jack told the reporters.

Making Taobao free was a key way to differentiate it from eBay, which collected fees from its users. We gambled that eBay would not match our move, since doing so would expose it to intense pressure from Wall Street investors who expected eBay to quickly capitalize on the $180 million it had already invested in the market. Sure enough, immediately after our press conference, journalists contacted eBay to ask if it, too, would offer free services. Caught off guard, eBay's local PR head responded by saying eBay would remain a website that charged, since charging for product listings and commissions was an important part of maintaining a healthy online marketplace. By the end of the day we had achieved our goal—we had backed eBay into a position that would be hard for it to change.

Taobao's "free for three years" marketing push helped attract new users. This was particularly important in China's low-trust environment, where people wanted to try something first before they had to pay for it. As our war of words heated up, eBay claimed to have a 95 percent share of the consumer market in China and pointed out to investors and media that eBay had never lost a market in which it had an established lead—the network effects of an online marketplace were simply too strong to overcome. However, eBay's 95 percent market share represented only the ten million Internet users in China who had actually tried e-commerce. Ninety-nine percent of China's population had yet to try buying anything online. And rather than try to attract eBay's sellers at first, we simply focused on everyone else. Because we already had millions of customers using our English-language site and domestic Chinese B2B site, Alibaba China, we had a ready customer base of sellers who could easily add a new retail business to their thriving wholesale business.

From day one, we recognized that making Taobao free was not enough. Sure, it would get people in the door. But we'd also have to keep them. Jack's message to the team was to forget everything about eBay's business model in the United States. It was more important, he argued, to focus on Chinese consumers and develop what they needed rather than what had worked in the United States.

The first step was recognizing that the consumer e-commerce model for China would not be an auction model, as at eBay. While eBay had gotten its start with people posting Pez dispensers and other consumer collectibles they had pulled out of their basements and put online for auction, China's consumer culture was entirely new. The Chinese did not have a hundred years of consumer products lying around in basements. After the poverty of the Cultural Revolution, no one had anything to collect, except for a few of Mao's little red books. What our customers really wanted, we realized, was simply a storefront for selling their products. Our goal was not to create a marketplace where multiple buyers could bid on one unique product posted online. It was to create a marketplace where multiple sellers could compete to offer the widest range of products and highest quality service to buyers who might otherwise shop for goods at the millions of small offline storefronts in China's nascent retail economy.

Working from this key insight, Taobao was vastly different from eBay China. Afraid that buyers and sellers might circumvent its system and avoid paying eBay's commissions, eBay went out of its way to keep buyers and sellers blind to each other and unable to communicate with one another before a purchase. This was a major inhibitor to commerce in an environment

where people were accustomed to building a personal relationship before doing business.

Our approach was exactly the opposite. Because we were entirely free, it didn't matter to us whether retailers consummated
their deals with buyers through our site. In fact, we encouraged
them to call each other, get to know each other, and even meet
face to face for large purchases. We were confident that, just as
we had found a way for Alibaba.com to make money from its
users without transaction fees, we ultimately would find a way
to make money from Taobao if its sellers were able to make
money. But first it was important to build a platform that gave
them *more* tools than they had offline rather than fewer.

To this end we decided to provide live chat software that
would allow buyers to contact sellers directly and communicate with them in real time. China was a nation crazy for chat
software, and we couldn't imagine commerce in China without
it. It would be like telling a retailer in the United States that
she couldn't have a telephone and would simply have to rely on
mail to communicate with her customers. So we introduced a
chat product called Wang Wang, complete with cute and flashy
emoticons. Buyers and sellers quickly adopted the chat software
as a part of the regular way they did business.

To eBay a service like Wang Wang would have been unthink-
able. Allowing buyers and sellers to chat in real time would have
torn apart eBay's entire business model. If people could haggle
and negotiate through chat, they could once again avoid paying
for eBay's product listing and transaction fees. But in a nation
where chat was a core part of the way young people used the
Internet, eBay was missing a major point.

Another major differentiation was the method of payment. Although the government had kept a tight rein on news and information domains on the Internet, officials had always been relatively hands-off about e-commerce. In fact the main rationale for allowing the Internet to expand in China was that it would bring economic benefits. So, as long as e-commerce companies operated responsibly, the government had been relatively encouraging. The one exception was online payments, which bled into the domain of China's highly regulated banking sector. E-commerce payments were very much a gray area, and there were no clear rules about whether and how companies could handle online payments. Jack recognized this problem and explained to me how he intended to approach it.

"The problem for online payments up until now is that there has not been any true standard for online payment to emerge in China. The reason is because each of the state-backed banks wants to create their own standard and so they are unwilling to cooperate with one another. But I've come up with the solution—we are going to create something called AliPay and then go out and sign up all the banks as partners."

He explained that what would make AliPay different from eBay's PayPal is that it would not provide direct payments between buyer and seller. Rather, it would be an escrow-based payment system, which would overcome the major barrier to e-commerce in China—lack of trust between buyer and seller. So, for example, after placing an order, a buyer would first send his money to an AliPay escrow account held by one of the banks. Then the seller would ship the product. Only after the buyer had inspected the product and verified that it arrived as described would the money be forwarded by AliPay to the seller's bank account.

"Actually, this wasn't an entirely new idea," Jack continued. "eBay once tried it in Korea but gave up on it. But we're pretty sure it will work here. And once AliPay grows large enough, we can slip in direct payments. And as our AliPay becomes more popular, someday it has the possibility to become China's largest bank."

As always, Jack was dreaming big.

THE GOOGLE GUYS

IT LOOKED TO BE JUST ANOTHER AVERAGE RAINY day in Hangzhou in fall 2004, so when the unexpected email hit my in-box, I instantly perked up. The Google Guys were coming to China, and they wanted to meet us.

Fresh off their record-shattering IPO the month before, the Google Guys—Larry Page and Sergey Brin—were the new billionaire heroes of the Internet industry. It was almost impossible to find a magazine that didn't feature them on the cover. Being called to meet them felt a bit like going to meet the Wizard of Oz, as a mysterious aura preceded them.

Having followed Google's development closely, we were in awe of them. But our awe was tempered by a healthy dose of fear. The Google Guys' visiting China could mean only one thing: Google was turning its attention to the China market. And in our worst nightmares we imagined a room of technicians in lab coats back at Google headquarters flipping an "Alibaba Killer" switch and—poof! Still, it was clear that when the Google Guys knock on your door, you'd better answer it. If there was any chance to have them on our side, rather than against us, we'd take it, so we agreed that Jack, Joe Tsai, and I would travel to Shanghai to meet the Google team in a private meeting room at the Grand Hyatt.

As I had ramped up our search advertising on Google, my admiration had only grown. Since my long week in quarantine I'd become obsessed with monitoring and growing our ad campaign. I found myself glued to the computer day and night, constantly checking Google ad reports to see how many new people we'd brought to the site each day, each hour, each minute. It was pretty amazing how, from a small apartment in the middle of China, we could coordinate a global marketing campaign. I was addicted to Google, stunned that something so simple could be so powerful.

Within a year our initial $600 budget had grown to $1 million, making us Google's largest advertiser in China. As our advertising budget grew, so did our relationship with the company, and in the spring of 2004 a colleague and I were flown to the Googleplex in Silicon Valley to speak to Google's employees about our experience with advertising on the site.

Traveling from Hangzhou to the Googleplex felt like going on a hajj to Mecca, and we knew it was a once-in-a-lifetime opportunity to see the epicenter of the Internet industry. As we walked through the sprawling modern campus of glass-and-steel buildings, Googlers played volleyball, Rollerbladed from building to building, and sat outside in shorts and sunglasses while sipping lattes and brainstorming the next great innovation. This other universe felt both parallel to and distant from China's rough-and-tumble Internet industry. If Alibaba's drab Hangzhou offices were like a broken-down Chevette, the shiny Googleplex was more like a glossy new Porsche. Both were technically cars, but beyond that there wasn't much similarity. I couldn't help but be impressed by the power contained in one office complex.

And so it was that five months later I found myself waiting in a Shanghai hotel lobby for Sergey and Larry. Joe and Jack were on their way, and, because I'd arrived much too early, I killed the time by pacing around the hotel lobby, staring out the windows at the Huangpu River, and trying to make out the colonial buildings along the Bund through the dense Shanghai smog. As I hadn't met the Google Guys on my trip to the Google headquarters, I was looking forward to finally meeting them and seeing what they were really like.

When Joe and Jack finally arrived, the three of us sat down to hammer out a strategy. The Google people had been vague about the purpose of the meeting, so we could only guess their intentions. We were privately wondering, perhaps even hoping, that Google was there to propose a major partnership or acquire us for a hefty sum. But we decided to play it safe. "Google called the meeting, so let's just go in and listen," Joe said. "No need to show all our cards."

We arrived at the meeting room, where we were greeted by some Google staffers and told to have a seat while the rest of the team returned from a break. As we looked around the room, it was clear that we were not the only people the Google honchos were meeting that day. Chairs were scattered around, and the large table was piled with loose documents and half-eaten snacks. I had envisioned a formal meeting to discuss potential partnerships, but it felt more like we were walking into an internal Google brainstorming session.

While we waited, we chatted with the staff, a mix of senior executives from international sales and operations. With the IPO behind them, they told us, they were turning their attention to international markets. Somewhat unnecessarily they also mentioned the private jet they'd chartered for this round-the-world trip.

Suddenly Larry Page entered the room, shook hands with us, and settled at one end of the table. I had read so much about him that I was expecting a charming, charismatic Internet pioneer, but my first impression was that he was more the classic tech geek. Hunched in his seat, he tended to look at the Google staffers, rather than us, as he spoke in his high-pitched monotone. His head and shoulders seemed to move as one fixed unit, making his mannerisms slightly robotic. Even his own colleagues seemed embarrassed by his style, which had an abrasive edge. Although an easy person to respect, he was a difficult one to warm up to.

Dispelling once and for all the hope that Google was in town to make an acquisition offer, Larry asked, "So what's Alibaba?"

It was clear that Larry had little idea of what we did, but Jack didn't seem to mind. He took a few minutes to walk the Google team through Alibaba's business and history. As always, Jack beamed with excitement, but the Google team— perhaps having heard the same type of story many times over the years—seemed indifferent.

We were still unclear about Google's intentions, so we asked for a bit more information about the purpose of the meeting. In response the Googlers embarked on a round of questions about our operations and revenue model.

"So where are most of your advertisers located? Only in the big cities or are they all around the country?"

"How do you sell to these customers? Do you use agents or sell directly?"

"How many people are on your sales team? How much do you pay them per month? What kind of commission do you provide them?"

At first we tried to answer as politely as possible, but as time went on the purpose of the meeting was becoming clear—we were being Googled. Stripped down and mined for data points to be fed into the Google machine. As the questions continued, fast and furious, I realized that Alibaba was just one in a series of companies whose executives the Google team was meeting with to suck out information that they would ultimately use against us.

I looked over at Jack to see his reaction. His smile had turned into a frown and he was sliding deeper into his chair. Reading his face, I could see that he was disappointed, even disgusted. Joe looked equally annoyed, and the meeting grew uncomfortable as our answers became increasingly defensive.

As one particularly sensitive question came up, I tried to lighten the mood by joking, "Well, we could tell you that, but we'd need to first have the secret Google search algorithm." Joe and Jack chuckled, but Larry and his team maintained their stone-faced expressions and continued their interrogation.

Perhaps sensing our growing discomfort, one of the junior Googlers cut in.

"Well, as you know, Alibaba is one of Google's largest advertisers in China, so we'd like to know how we're doing and how we can improve."

Since I managed the Google advertising campaigns, Joe and Jack turned to me. "Well, compared to Yahoo!, we love

Google's technology and, most of all, the results we get," I told them. "But we've been happier about the service we're getting on Yahoo!. The team takes a bit more time to work with us to make sure we run smart campaigns."

Larry cut in, joking, "Why don't you get your service from Yahoo! but spend your money on Google?"

I looked at Jack, who was plainly astonished. Although it was ostensibly just a (lame) joke, Larry's response revealed a fundamental difference between Google, the technology company, and Alibaba, the service company. Like Yahoo!, Alibaba was proud of using human editors from the beginning, in keeping with Jack's declaration: "We are not an Internet company, we are a service company." Google, on the other hand, believed that nearly everything could be automated, including customer service. Given this divide, it was not surprising that Jack seemed to hit it off much better with Jerry Yang, the Yahoo! founder, than with the Google Guys.

Just as the meeting began to stall, Sergey Brin, munching on an apple, walked into the room. He greeted us and, rather than joining us at the table, paced around the room, jumping into the conversation between bites. Dressed casually, his dark hair blown back from his pointy face, he looked as if he had just walked out of a Frisbee game on a Stanford quad. His informal, energetic style seemed to have been shaped more by Silicon Valley than his Russian homeland. At first Sergey seemed an odd match for Larry, who looked like he got more light from his computer screen than California's sunny skies. But as Sergey spoke, it became clear that behind his casual exterior was a focused and determined mind that loved to chew on complex problems.

"So what were we all talking about before I arrived?" he asked.

Jack repeated some of the top-level information about the company as Sergey paced around the room. Sergey was clearly the people person of the duo, although the way he walked around the room—as if he was in charge of the meeting—had an air of arrogance. But despite their style differences, Jack seemed to warm up to Sergey, and the tone of the meeting became much friendlier. After a while Sergey sat down, and the discussion moved toward government regulation of the Internet in China.

We all knew that when Google looked at the Chinese market, it faced a dilemma, particularly in regard to censorship. Despite having no physical presence on the ground, Google's services had grown quickly in China through word of mouth. But Google's road in China had been bumpy, and the service was occasionally blocked by China's firewall. If Google truly wanted to become a leader in China, it would have to set up local operations and build a local team, which meant following local laws.

From my previous discussions with Google employees, I knew that, within the company, no one agreed about how to approach the issue of censorship. While I respected and admired Google's views on corporate social responsibility, which simply stated, "Don't be evil," I also realized that in China things are not always so black and white.

Sergey was the first to begin talking about the issue.

"We're still working out how to set up our websites for China," he said. "Obviously the issue of China's firewall is an important one for us. What do you think the government's response would be if we simply allowed Google's search results to appear unfiltered and then the China government's own fire-wall would take down politically sensitive search results? Ideally that's the way we'd like to have it, so that we are not actively doing the filtering."

Jack shook his head. "I know what you're saying, but the government will never accept that."

"Why?"

"From the government's point of view, that's like if you go to a country, walk along the street, and throw litter all around and expect the police to follow you and pick up after you."

The Google team looked disappointed. Sergey suggested a number of different scenarios that, Google executives hoped, might allow them to operate their China business without censoring content. But in Jack's view none of those ideas would meet the basic requirement of following the local laws.

"Look," Jack said, "the China government is very supportive of the Internet. I've been doing Internet businesses since 1995, and I've never had someone come in and say, 'Jack, you can't do this or you can't do that.' If you come to China and your business is helping create jobs for people, if you are helping society, they will support you. But if you are running a business in China, you'll be expected to follow the local laws. That's the same for every company in every country."

The Google team appeared sullen. Self-censoring content was clearly a tough idea for them to accept. Google's stated mission was "to organize the world's information and make it universally accessible and useful." Inherent in this mission was the idea that making information universally accessible would bring economic, social, and even political power to people at a grassroots level.

For a few moments the room was silent as the Google team mulled the options. The silence was broken when a Google staffer let us know the time was up. As we shook hands, I realized that it would probably take a while before Google worked through the ethical issues involved in doing business in China. But I also knew they'd find a way eventually, and when they did, we'd better be ready.

CROCODILE IN THE YANGTZE

MILITARY HELICOPTERS BUZZED OVERHEAD AS A row of tanks clinked across the battlefield, destroying everything in sight. A team of elite soldiers weaved and dodged past explosions and enemy fire while advancing toward the enemy stronghold.

"The enemy is within our sights," came a voice over the loudspeaker. "Fire when ready!"

With a flash a helicopter missile streamed through the air, leaving a smoky plume behind it as it headed toward the enemy compound.

Boom! Crash! Rat-a-tat-tat. The enemy compound burst into flames.

"Enemy destroyed! The Taobao militia has seized a strategic new beachhead," bellowed the narrator. "Taobao's advance is unstoppable!"

THE VIDEO ENDED and triumphant military music filled the auditorium as the lights came on. The audience clapped and cheered, filled with the sense that, as Alibaba entered 2005, we had the winds of victory at our backs. It was our annual all-hands kickoff meeting, and we had plenty of reason to cheer for the Year of the Rooster.

Taobao had had a phenomenal year in 2004, and we'd made significant headway against eBay in China. Our strategy to engage eBay in a war of words had created a lot of media buzz within China. Positioning ourselves as a local David fighting the US Goliath, we intended to educate the market about e-commerce and attract people to Taobao to give consumer e-commerce a chance.

We'd overcome some major challenges from eBay's superior firepower and resources. Hoping to lock Taobao out of the market, eBay had negotiated exclusive advertising deals with all of the major Internet portals in China. But to do this, they'd paid a premium to have Taobao excluded from advertising on the portals. To overcome this direct attack, we'd taken the guerilla approach of negotiating tiny advertising deals with hundreds of small websites throughout China who were more than happy to provide a price discount to the prevailing online advertising rates in China. They were simply grateful to have any advertiser at all. This, along with some aerial assaults in the form of television advertising and outdoor display ad campaigns, had been showing great results at only a fraction of the amount that eBay was spending.

Taobao was growing quickly on all metrics. While eBay charged for product listings, Taobao had kept its website free. The result: Taobao surpassed eBay's product listing numbers. With more products on the site for customers to browse, Taobao's website traffic had increased beyond eBay's. And as

Taobao's traffic increased, eBay PowerSellers (high-volume sellers with top reputations), who had initially resisted moving to Taobao, had no choice but to open a second shop on Taobao. On nearly all metrics, Taobao was surpassing eBay, giving us the right to boast that Taobao was "China's largest online consumer marketplace" and build even greater momentum with customers.

Admittedly this marketing-speak hid one important fact. By the end of 2004 we were still trailing eBay on the key metric by which media and analysts measured marketplaces: gross merchandise volume (GMV), or the total sales carried out on the site. But even here the numbers looked promising. Although we had begun 2004 with a 9 percent market share of GMV versus eBay's 90 percent, we ended 2004 with a 41 percent market share versus eBay's 53 percent. While media and analysts outside China were still favoring eBay to prevail, we had gained enough confidence internally to feel we were on the right track.

With the kickoff meeting audience at full tilt, Jack took the stage.

"2004 was a great year for us all, and we should be really proud of what we achieved so far. There are only two companies in the world who truly understand how to build an e-commerce marketplace—Alibaba and eBay. And last year we showed the market that we understand China much better than eBay does. But as we say at Alibaba, last year's result is next year's minimum level of achievement. And don't forget: we don't want Taobao to be just the largest consumer marketplace in China. We want it to be the largest in the world!"

The crowd applauded wildly as Jack stepped off the stage and handed the microphone to Toto Sun, the head of Taobao.

"Thanks, Jack, for giving us all your support. And Jack's right, because we are going to beat eBay. Because I know one thing: when the foreign devils come to China, they will definitely be killed!"

I stood at the back of the auditorium and smiled as the crowd laughed and clapped. I recognized the old Red Army rallying cry, and I knew it was meant as a harmless joke. But moments like that did make me wonder whether this kind of ironic distance could become harmful in the long term. So I was relieved when Jack immediately jumped on stage and took the microphone back from Toto.

"There's one thing I want to be clear about here," Jack said. "Our war is just a fun competition with eBay, and this is nothing about nationality. Alibaba is a global company, and we have international staff here from America, Europe, and other places. So I don't want to hear any kind of nationalistic talk. This is a game. It's a sport. We are lucky to have a big competitor like eBay. It's like we have the chance to play basketball against Michael Jordan."

Having made his point, Jack handed the microphone back to Toto. Humbled, Toto resumed his speech. I was pleased that Jack had stepped in to rein in the rhetoric before it got out of hand, even at the expense of a senior manager's pride (no small thing in Chinese culture). Toto was a great colleague and friend, but his words could easily have taken on a life of their own. And I'd always been proud that Alibaba's success was based on innovation and merit rather than nationalistic rhetoric.

We in China knew the incredible progress Taobao was making, but halfway around the world eBay had the media and its investors convinced that it was still the leading marketplace in China. Small wonder—the notion that the world's largest e-commerce company could be successfully challenged by a local Chinese upstart would have sounded ludicrous to the media and analysts covering eBay at the time. eBay kicked off 2005 with a day of wooing analysts; Meg Whitman used the annual Analyst Day to put a positive spin on eBay's growth in China while explaining the additional investment of $100 million they had recently made in the market:

"Today eBay Eachnet is by far the number one e-commerce site in China. We're helping China to define its e-commerce future, and it gives me tremendous satisfaction to see eBay Eachnet helping so many young Chinese taste entrepreneurship for the first time.

"Now, like in the early days of the Net in the United States and other countries, there are a bunch of small competitors in China nipping at our heels, and I don't blame them. They see the opportunity too, but guess what? We love competition. Absolutely love it. We have from the earliest days. It motivates us. It makes us hungry. It makes us stronger, and it makes us very, very determined. We are on a tear to be the undisputed winner in China, and the additional $100 million investment we announced last month should be a sign of an unmistakable commitment and an unstoppable determination to win that market. . . . Just as we pulled ahead of able competitors in the US and Germany in 1999 and 2000, we're pulling farther ahead in China today . . . The share of e-commerce in China is likely to be the defining measure of business success on the net."[1]

Despite her positive spin on eBay's position in China, behind the scenes we heard that eBay truly was becoming concerned about Eachnet's performance. Someone who had attended one of eBay's board meetings told us that eBay's market research was showing that, on a head-to-head comparison, eBay was falling behind Taobao on nearly every metric. When it came to customer service, user satisfaction, renewal rates, and other important metrics, eBay ranked higher only on its number of registered users. And Taobao was quickly gaining ground. eBay's growth story in China was central to its investor presentations, and the company must have been concerned that Eachnet would be revealed as a paper tiger if eBay didn't move quickly to shore up its market position in China. By committing an additional $100 million to the China market, mostly earmarked for advertising, eBay was doubling down in an attempt to both demonstrate its commitment to China and intimidate us.

But eBay's dismissal of Taobao as a legitimate competitor only inspired us to reach higher. And we recognized that having a great site that fit the China market was more important than any PR or marketing strategy. And on this front eBay seemed to be playing right into our hands, appearing to make the kind of blunders that any first-year student at Harvard Business School, Meg Whitman's MBA alma mater, could have foreseen.

Upon acquiring the rest of Eachnet, eBay's first step—and its first colossal mistake—was to link its China platform to its US platform. eBay's thinking was that in order to build a global marketplace, it should have every country in the world working from the same platform. To make this transition, eBay froze all local website development in order to prepare for the migration of its data and technology to the global platform. In doing so, eBay eliminated localized features and functions that Chinese Internet users enjoyed and forced them to use the same platform that had been popular in the United States and Germany.

Most likely, eBay executives figured that because the platform had thrived in more industrialized markets, its technology and functionality must be superior to a platform from a developing country. The inherent arrogance was not unlike what I'd seen from the international managers in Hong Kong who had shunned Alibaba's website for lacking sophistication.

The response from Eachnet users was instant disaster for eBay. Customers flocked to Taobao, saying that eBay's new cold minimalist interface lacked Taobao's more intangible human feeling, with its cute icons and flashing animations. An additional issue was that, where user names overlapped, eBay had given priority to its international members and forced its China users to give up their user names and register new accounts. This problem proved to be more common than eBay had anticipated, creating confusion for eBay's PowerSellers in China, because the online ratings they had acquired over time were now reset to zero, and their loyal customers could no longer find them online. eBay's customers in China took to its message boards to complain about what they perceived as unfair treatment. Finally, eBay had failed to account for the China firewall, which slowed down Internet speeds between the United States and China. Although e-commerce was considered politically neutral and not censored, the firewall still meant that accessing international websites from China was slower than accessing China-based websites. This was something we'd encountered with Alibaba.com; to resolve the issue we had set up mirror servers in both the United States and China. eBay's failure to anticipate the problem had led to poor website performance.

Aside from the immediate issues, the transition set eBay on a course for long-term problems. This was clear to us because of our own early mistake of moving our website operations to Silicon Valley. By making Chinese product developers report to executives in Silicon Valley, any minor bit of customization, such as changing the color of a button, required approval from California. Given the time difference, which allowed for only one hour of overlap between the working days of the United States and China, we knew that eBay's decision would lead to a huge rift between the China team—which wanted to move quickly in a dynamic market—and the US team, which was serving a much more mature platform.

Another important part of our strategy was to stir up eBay's US investors about its performance. Our "last person standing" strategy had worked for Alibaba. And we knew it could work against eBay as well. If we could convince Wall Street that eBay was burning through cash while losing ground to Taobao, we could test the patience of eBay's investors. And we gambled that eBay would eventually succumb to the pressure to show results instead of playing the long game.

We called up the one journalist who knew Alibaba well enough to actually take our claims about our performance seriously—Justin Doebele, whose July 2000 article had put Alibaba on the cover of *Forbes* magazine. Justin had seen Jack and Alibaba at its scrappiest and watched as we beat our US B2B competitors despite all sorts of skepticism. So, almost five years after he'd first visited us in Hangzhou to chronicle our B2B battles, we invited Justin up to Hangzhou, took him out on a boat on the West Lake, and shared all the data about our battle with eBay.

"We want to be the world's largest consumer site," Jack told Justin. "eBay may be a shark in the ocean, but I am a crocodile in the Yangtze River. If we fight in the ocean, we lose—but if we fight in the river, we win." A few weeks later *Forbes* ran Justin's story, "Standing Up to a Giant"—the first time a major publication had suggested that eBay was not doing so well in China. We had finally landed a serious body blow and awakened mainstream US investors to the plight of eBay in China. eBay would soon feel the pressure.

THE EBAY-
ALIBABA HOTLINE

ON AN UNUSUALLY CLEAR DAY IN MAY 2005 THE
Fortune Global Forum kicked off at the Diaoyutai State Guest-
house in Beijing. The bright sun bounced off the glossy red pil-
lars, green trim, and golden tile roof of the Chinese hotel as
guests filtered into the main hall. When it opened in 1959, the
Diaoyutai's guests were diplomats and heads of state of Mao's
Communist allies. But times had changed, and it was now host
to the world's leading capitalists, who had descended upon Beijing to network and curry favor with government leaders, including China's president, Hu Jintao, who was delivering the
keynote address.

Among those capitalists were Jack Ma and Meg Whitman.
It was the first time they had appeared at a conference together
in China, and the media were waiting to see whether sparks
would fly between the two rivals.

As I strolled into the venue with Jack, he let me in on a
secret.

"Porter, tomorrow night Joe and I are going to be having a private dinner with Meg Whitman and her communications chief, Henry Gomez. I haven't told you this, but eBay has expressed an interest in buying Taobao."

My eyes lit up. eBay acquiring Taobao? This could be huge.

"So what have they said so far?"

"They contacted us last year and wanted to meet with us. So we visited eBay's offices to get a feel for each other. As I walked around, there were a few Chinese engineers who recognized me. But so far nobody else knows. They gave us an initial offer, but it was way too low for us to even consider. So we're meeting with them again tomorrow night to hear what they have to say this time."

This is getting interesting, I thought. *eBay must really be starting to get nervous.*

"Should we go and have a look at the venue?" Jack asked. "I want to know what to expect."

Jack and I walked over to the conference hall for Jack's speech and instantly spotted Meg Whitman. Tall, confident, and with a big smile, she walked over.

"Hi, Jack. Great to see you again. We came a bit early so that we could hear your speech."

"Oh, hi, Meg," Jack responded. "Welcome to Beijing. I'm looking forward to hearing your speech as well."

Laughing and chatting, the two seemed like good friends reuniting. There was no sense of bad blood, despite our highly public battle.

Jack introduced me. "This is Porter. He's in charge of our international PR." I shook hands with Meg and exchanged a few friendly words. Standing next to her and dwarfed by her height was eBay's communications chief, Henry Gomez. I introduced myself to Henry and we did our best to banter politely. We were interrupted when a photographer wandered over, having spied Meg and Jack standing together. Before the photographer could take a shot, Henry slid between the two CEOs. I could only assume he wanted to prevent any public speculation that eBay and Alibaba might be discussing a partnership.

Jack took the stage and gave an uncharacteristically flat talk. I had expected him to deliver a home run, but I guess he was distracted by having Meg in the audience. After all, even if Taobao was drawing neck and neck with eBay in China, we were still very much in its shadow on the world stage.

After Jack's talk we exchanged some more pleasantries, and Henry and I exchanged cards.

"We should go to lunch while you're here," I suggested.

"Sure, how about tomorrow at my hotel?" Henry replied. And our date was set.

The next day I met Henry in the lobby of the St. Regis. I was both nervous and excited. It felt a bit like the head propagandists of the United States and Soviet Union were sitting down for a secret meal at the peak of the Cold War.

I hadn't quite decided on how to approach the lunch. On the one hand, eBay was our mortal enemy. On the other hand, if we got acquired, there was a good chance that I might be working closely with Henry. *Better not to be too antagonistic,* I thought. *I'll keep it friendly.*

"I have to hand it to you. You guys have done a good job of making our life difficult lately," Henry began. "We're at a bit of a disadvantage in China because of the time zone difference and the fact that we're a publicly listed company. We can't just instantly respond whenever a journalist comes to us with a question."

It was true, something we had exploited when making competitive announcements. We knew that making announcements at midday in China would mean eBay was still asleep in the US. Bound by the constraints of being a public company, any response from eBay's China team would require approval from eBay in California. Putting this sort of full-court press on eBay was the most effective way to make them look slow-footed.

"Well, we do our best," I replied. "There's one thing you should know about Jack Ma. He's easily underestimated. He plays business like a game of chess."

"So how many people do you have on your PR team?" he asked.

"Oh, just me for international and then one other guy for domestic PR."

He seemed surprised. I knew they were already working with a large agency in China.

"So one of the things I've wondered about," he continued, "is that you've been making a lot of boasts about your data. And, you know, we've been through that before with another competitor in Germany. They were faking their data, and ultimately they were exposed and fizzled out."

I was surprised that he thought we might be faking our data. It showed that he still didn't quite believe we were catching up with eBay.

"I can tell you that we're 100 percent clean on our data," I said. "We take it very seriously. We're gearing up to be a public company someday, so we follow very strict standards on that."

"So what do you do about counterfeit products on the site?" he asked. His tone seemed to imply he thought we were not doing enough. And, admittedly, we probably were not. Although we met the US standard for notice and take down of counterfeit goods, operating in China meant there were simply more counterfeiters to contend with and so it was all too easy to find fake products listed by small merchants on Taobao. I had always argued we should be doing more than simply meeting the legal standard. We should be pioneering the solution, I believed.

"We have the same policy as eBay," I replied. "If we're notified of fakes on the site, we take them down." Henry nodded expressionlessly. In the back of my mind I knew that it was a PR issue we were vulnerable on, especially as a Chinese company.

As we wrapped up, he probed one last issue.

"You know, one of the things we've noticed is a tone of nationalism in what you guys are saying. And that's the one thing we don't think is fair. Neither of us should be playing the nationalism card."

Could he really be missing the whole point of our PR? I wondered. We weren't arguing that we'd win because US companies didn't deserve to win. Our argument was that by arrogantly bringing its US model to the China market, and even sending in international managers from Korea and Germany to run the China operations, eBay was not in a position to build a product that truly fit the local market. I told the story of how Jack had jumped on stage to interrupt Toto after he'd made an inappropriate nationalistic comment.

"Okay, that makes me feel better," Henry responded. "Let's all agree that we don't play the nationalism card."

"Why don't we create a hotline, so that if things get too heated, we can be in touch to diffuse the situation?" I suggested.

"Okay, I like that idea," he said. "Let's keep in touch."

We shook hands and parted ways. It had been a cordial conversation but not without an edge. I was curious to see where it would lead.

A few weeks later we got a sense of where things were headed when a number of anti-Japanese postings referencing Softbank's stake in Alibaba began surfacing on eBay China, Taobao, and other bulletin boards. We suspected eBay had a role in propagating the protests. The postings coincided with nationwide protests in China about a recent diplomatic incident involving China and Japan. The anti-Japanese protests, while initially quietly encouraged by the Chinese government, had spiraled out of hand. And as Chinese took to the streets, the government had started to clamp down. Nevertheless the nastiness posed a risk to Taobao—if Taobao could be labeled as a Japanese company, China's netizens might decide to abandon us.

At about this time, Henry activated the hotline by sending me a sharply worded email asking about rumors circulating in China that Meg was relocating to Shanghai for six months to run the eBay China business and replace the Chinese leadership team with Americans. Suggesting Alibaba was behind the rumor, he raised a warning: "Given the majority investment in Alibaba of a Japanese company, I think we should avoid going down the nationalism road."

We, too, had read that Meg was coming to China, but after I checked around inside Alibaba, we were convinced that no one within our team had spread the word. I wrote back to try to calm Henry:

Henry,

Thanks for the email. . . .

As for the rumors, the rumors cited below look so ridiculous I can't imagine any Chinese or foreign media taking them seriously. . . .

On nationalism—as I mentioned it is against our policy to play any nationalism card. But there are very good business arguments for why Chinese management and a Chinese company have advantages in understanding customers on a Chinese-language website. No American Internet company is in the lead in China (although you may disagree). This has more to do with product localization and speed to market than anything—reporting back to the US usually slows things down, as you mentioned in our lunch. We always keep it to a business rationale rather than something very base like "Don't use eBay because it is American." We'd never say that.

Japan—I didn't really mention this at our lunch, but we have seen lots of Japan-related postings on Taobao, even posted on the eBay China website. We have some guesses where many of these are coming from. . . . I'm sure you'll agree that "nationalism" has more to do with raising political or cultural issues and playing up anti-whoever sentiment. I can assure you we don't go there.

If I was really sneaky I'd encourage you to play up the Japan issue. As you may already know, the Chinese government banned anti-Japan bulletin boards, boycott efforts, etc. after the recent protests in China. There was even a huge crackdown on Internet sites. I'm not sure how the Chinese government would take to any internet company supporting efforts against Japan. We stay away from these political winds because they change too quickly in China.

Henry—we have a lot of fun competition coming up. I look forward to it.

Cheers,
Porter

Henry responded with a sterner email, warning us that while China was calling for restraint against anti-Japan protests: "Chinese consumers might still want to know more about the origins of your company. . . . There's always a way to get the message out." He finished with a boast: "It's going to be fun solidifying our #1 position in the market. We have $100 million worth of excitement and a few more surprises coming right at you. I hope Jack's investors are ready to cough up more cash, again! :-)"

It was a not-so-veiled threat, along with some sophomoric chest thumping. It deserved nothing more than sophomoric trash talk in return. So I wrote him back with a recommendation for two books he might find useful for his summer reading: *The Search for Modern China* and *Building a Website for Dummies*. I never heard back.

Although we hadn't started the rumor about Meg's spending six months in China, it soon became clear that there was a degree of truth to it as Meg and Henry were spending more time in Shanghai, trying to fix their China problem. And if Meg and Henry were bringing the fight to us on our home turf in Shanghai, we had only one choice—to take the fight to eBay in its home town of San Jose. As we planned our offensive, the timing couldn't have been better. eBay was set to host its ten-year anniversary party for all its customers and employees at its annual eBay Live! event. Alibaba would be represented; earlier in the year eBay had approved a booth for Alibaba.com in the vendor services section of eBay Live!. With an expected attendance of more than 10,000 members of the eBay community, it was a great chance for us to both market Alibaba.com's services to eBay's PowerSellers and pressure eBay to sweeten its offer for Taobao. To achieve both goals we had to find a way to create a buzz about Taobao among eBay's members in the US.

eBay's decision to allow Alibaba.com a booth at eBay Live! was a welcome goodwill gesture, and Alibaba.com's presence there would have made sense for both companies. Although Taobao and eBay China were in an intense battle in China, Alibaba.com and eBay were actually quite complementary businesses in the US. Alibaba's marketplace hosted tens of thousands of Chinese wholesalers who sold products that America's consumers wanted. eBay's PowerSellers were constantly looking for new products to offer to their customers. Theoretically the idea of "buy on Alibaba, sell on eBay" made sense. Hooking Alibaba's wholesalers up with eBay's PowerSellers would have generated more transactions on eBay's marketplaces, driving eBay's revenues even higher.

But in order to hurt Alibaba, eBay was willing to suffer. At the eleventh hour eBay reversed its decision and said Alibaba could not have a booth at the event. Then eBay took it one step further and gave the booth space to Alibaba's B2B archnemesis, Global Sources, and announced that the two companies had formed a simple partnership, which immediately sent Global

Sources' stock up 50 percent. With Global Sources its new partner, eBay said there was no room for an Alibaba booth at the
event.

But uninviting us to eBay's party only strengthened our resolve to make our presence known to eBay's customers at eBay
Live!. We spent weeks quietly preparing for the event. First we
booked presidential suites at two hotels adjoining the McEnery
Convention Center, the venue for eBay Live!. Next we ordered
thousands of huge bright-orange swag bags emblazoned with
the Alibaba logo. Finally, we bought ads on popular blogs read
by eBay's PowerSellers.

On the day of the event we caught eBay completely off guard.
As thousands of eBay users poured into the venue, they received
their bright-orange Alibaba bags, creating a sea of bright Alibaba orange inside the arena. eBay's staff called security to try to
shut down the operation, but eBay could do nothing to stem the
tide of orange because Alibaba's staff had made sure to distribute the bags just outside the perimeter of the convention center,
on public land. Meanwhile we made sure that the bloggers who
followed eBay were well aware of eBay's strong-arm tactics. As
word of the conflict reached conference attendees, eBay learned
the hard way that the only relationship stronger than the relationship between eBay and its customers was the relationship
that its customers had with each other. eBay's efforts to lock
Alibaba out of its event fed into a growing resentment among
its customers at eBay's efforts to keep its entire ecosystem closed
to outsiders. "Why keep out a service that can only help eBay
customers?" the chorus went. Sympathetic to Alibaba's cause,
eBay Live! attendees encouraged each other to attend the Alibaba seminars at our hotel suites. If eBay had simply allowed us

to participate with a booth as originally planned, we would not have ramped up our marketing efforts, and they would not have had nearly as much impact. But as it turned out, eBay helped promote Alibaba while creating a minirevolt within its own community.

eBay's frustration was evident when it held its annual shareholder meeting ten minutes away in Santa Clara, shortly after the eBay Live! event. When asked by an attendee about her view of Alibaba, Meg Whitman sniped that Alibaba had a serious problem with counterfeit goods. But the remark failed to hurt Alibaba and instead was regarded as a hypocritical cheap shot, with the prominent eBay watcher Ina Steiner calling the comment "ironic given eBay suffers from that problem too"[1] and had been sued by Tiffany & Company over the problem of counterfeit goods.

Our US offensive had paid off. To all of eBay's key audience—media, analysts, investors, and customers—Meg Whitman was losing control of the story. Not only was eBay's status in China sinking, but the damage was beginning to find its way back to the company's home turf. To stop the bleeding eBay came back to the bargaining table with a sweetened offer for Taobao. But Jack had a move that eBay had not anticipated.

YAHOO!

"PORTER, THERE'S AN URGENT MEETING DOWN-stairs that Jack needs you to attend," Jack's assistant told me as we entered the summer of 2005.

"What's it about?" I asked.

"He'll tell you at the meeting. But all of the senior managers need to be there. You should go downstairs right away."

At the meeting room I found the entire senior management team sitting around a table. A sudden meeting such as this could mean only one of two things—very good news or very bad news.

Jack walked in, put his hands on the table, and got straight to the point.

"I've got a big announcement everyone—we're buying Yahoo! China."

The team was surprised. Shocked, even. We hadn't seen that coming. And if *we* hadn't seen it, one thing was for sure— neither would eBay.

Jack explained how the deal had come about. "A few weeks ago I was at a conference in Pebble Beach, and I started chatting with Jerry Yang. We started talking about what we could do together in China. I told him that if he really wanted Yahoo! to win in China, he should let us run it. After talking with them for a few weeks, we agreed in principle to a deal, and now we're finalizing it. Yahoo!'s going to invest $1 billion in Alibaba and we're going to take over Yahoo! China."

Yahoo! wasn't the most obvious choice for a partner, but the more Jack explained the rationale for the deal, the more sense it made. Since becoming the first US Internet company to enter the China market in 1999, Yahoo! had struggled through a series of partnerships, none of which had worked out. But its early entrance into China had given Yahoo! an advantage—its executives had learned from their six years of mistakes. Chief among these lessons was that they could not simply apply their US model to the China market. They quickly found that translating international content for the China market didn't satisfy the needs of local consumers, and Yahoo!'s growth had failed to keep pace with that of local rivals who had developed features and content that better fit the China market.

In 2003 Yahoo! attempted to rectify the problem by acquiring local search engine leader 3721, led by the feisty entrepreneur Zhou Hongyi. The main driver of 3721's growth was controversial antivirus software Zhou had created that, once downloaded, also installed a search toolbar on the computers of Internet users that defaulted to the 3721 search engine. Within the industry the 3721 software was widely regarded as a "hooligan application," since it often installed without the user's being fully aware and was quite difficult to uninstall. Nevertheless Zhou's aggressive tactics worked; 3721 quickly became the second-largest search engine in China, and in 2003 Yahoo! bought it, keeping Zhou on to head Yahoo! China's business. Over time, however, a rift grew between Zhou Hongyi and Yahoo's US management, and Yahoo! began to look for alternatives for doing business in China.

In the process Yahoo! looked to the example of Yahoo! Japan, where the company had partnered with Alibaba's main investor, Softbank. Japan was the one market in which Yahoo! didn't actually control its local business. Instead it owned a minority share and let Softbank run Yahoo! Japan through a licensing arrangement. Yahoo!'s decision to put a local partner in charge of Yahoo! Japan had allowed Yahoo! Japan to thrive by generating localized content that better fit Japan's unique local conditions, leading Yahoo! Japan into a solid market leadership position.

Yahoo! Japan also had the distinction of being the only company to have beaten eBay in a major market. eBay had entered the market after Yahoo! Japan and withdrew from the Japanese market in 2002. So from Yahoo!'s perspective, striking a deal with us meant it could solve its China management problem and gain a foothold in China's growing e-commerce space, backing a team that had a chance of beating eBay in China, just as Softbank's Yahoo! Japan had won the auction market in Japan.

From Alibaba's perspective the upside was not as clear. On paper eBay seemed like the more logical partner, with marketplace models that clearly complemented ours. Plugging Taobao into eBay's global portfolio would have fit the Chinese market snugly into eBay's global embrace, leaving only Japan out of its worldwide network. And Alibaba's B2B businesses would have been the last piece of the puzzle, connecting the world's manufacturers, trading companies, and wholesalers with eBay's PowerSellers.

On the other hand, Alibaba partnering with a search engine leader would create an entirely new business model, one that combined marketplaces and a search engine under one roof. In US terms it would be like combining eBay, PayPal, Yahoo!, and Google in one entity. Partnering with Yahoo! would safeguard us against the rise of search engine advertising, which we feared would siphon ad revenue from Alibaba and Taobao as Internet users became more savvy and abandoned our platforms to create their own websites which they'd then promote on search engines. We were already losing some of our customers' advertising dollars to Google and Baidu, the major Chinese search engine. And we knew from our meeting with the Google founders that they probably would be making an aggressive push into China soon. Why compete against search engines, Jack thought, when you can own one yourself?

The decision came down to Jack's desire to take on the bigger challenge. Nine times out of ten, an entrepreneur would have gone with eBay, just as Eachnet's founder, Shao Yibo, had done. But to Jack joining eBay seemed almost too simple, too predictable. On the other hand, buying a search engine and entering the hottest growth area of the Internet? That was a move no one would expect.

It also helped that Yahoo! gave us a partner who spoke the same language—literally. While Jack liked Meg Whitman personally, he believed she simply wanted to buy the Chinese market rather than build something that would truly benefit entrepreneurs in China over the long term. But the cofounder of Yahoo!, the Taiwanese American Jerry Yang, had a great working relationship with Jack. With common language and cultural roots, the two hit it off the first time they met, back in 1997, when Jack was still working for the government in Beijing. Jack had been assigned to show Jerry around, and they visited the Great Wall together. According to Jack, Jerry had even suggested Jack should join Yahoo! as the head of its China operations.

Jerry's Taiwanese roots also helped open doors with the Chinese government. His familiarity with the culture and language provided some assurance to the government that Yahoo! would be a more accommodating partner than the average Western business. Hailing from Taiwan was not as politically correct as hailing from mainland China, but at least it seemed less foreign. Jerry had been an inspiration to Chinese entrepreneurs and, despite his company's struggles, still had the halo of being the first Chinese American to have made it big on the Internet.

But one reason above all led to the deal. "For us this deal is all about search," Jack explained. "We are going to be the only company in the world that brings B2B marketplaces, consumer marketplaces, payment, and search engines together in one company."

If the structure of the deal was ambitious, the scale was staggering. Under the terms that had been drafted, Yahoo! would invest $1 billion in Alibaba Group and hand over its Yahoo! China operations. In exchange it would receive a 40 percent stake in Alibaba Group, valuing Alibaba at just over $4 billion. It was going to be one of the largest Internet deals in history and put Alibaba in the global spotlight.

"By the way, your shares are now worth $6.50 per share," Jack told us at the meeting. The room let out a collective gasp. It was four times what we'd expected the shares to be worth. "And everyone in the company will have the opportunity to sell 25 percent of their shares at that price if the deal closes. It means we won't have an IPO for a while, but it will at least give everyone a taste of the fruits of their labor." It was exciting to think we were finally going to have a chance to see the value of our hard work and that the stock options we had on paper might actually be worth something. Allowing us to sell only 25 percent was a wise move by Jack and Joe Tsai, as it allowed staff members to taste the potential while leaving enough incentive for them to stay with the company for the long term. For myself, it created a personal milestone as well—five years after I first daydreamed about becoming a millionaire, it would finally happen. Rather than coming as a result of a long-planned IPO, my millionaire status had arrived when I least expected it. I took a deep breath and thought about what it would mean for my life.

"We have a lot of work to do before we announce the deal, and it's still not finalized," Jack went on. "The HR team is going to have a lot to prepare for, bringing in Yahoo! China to the Alibaba family. And PR is going to be extra busy. Porter, we're going to need you to come out to Yahoo!'s headquarters as we finalize the deal, to help draft the announcement."

A few weeks later I was walking down University Avenue in Palo Alto, California, just down a palm-lined street from the Spanish arches of my alma mater. I'd graduated in the Stanford class of 1992, into a recession. I had never used the Internet (few people had; commercial use of the Internet was only about a year old) and was unsure where my career might take me. The class just behind me generated the first batch of Internet millionaires, who stumbled into jobs at Yahoo! and Excite in their earliest days. But by the time the Internet really began to take off in the US, I was already in China. Now it had brought me back to Palo Alto, ten years after Jerry Yang and David Filo had first registered the domain Yahoo.com for their search engine. It was a homecoming made even sweeter by the thought that Alibaba would be joining forces with Yahoo!—the granddaddy of them all.

I met with Jack, Joe, and the rest of the deal team for dinner. They'd been working around the clock on the negotiations, and I quickly learned that although they'd agreed on broad strokes (in principle), the actual details were an entirely different matter. Joe and the lawyers had already gone several complicated rounds with Yahoo!, and a few sticking points remained. One was the sensitive question of how to announce the deal to best ensure its acceptance by the Chinese government.

Yahoo!'s goal was to create the perception that it was acquiring Alibaba. With a market value of roughly $40 billion, Yahoo! wanted to be seen by investors as aggressively expanding into China, rather than giving up on the China market and handing over its operations to a local company. Yahoo! executives seemed to think that the latter would make them look weak.

This goal was entirely at odds with our own. In our view positioning the deal as Yahoo!'s acquiring Alibaba was not only inaccurate. It put the future of Alibaba at risk in China by creating the perception that Alibaba was now under full control of Yahoo!, an American company. This would put us at a disadvantage with local government and partners on every issue, from gaining licenses to setting up new offices and research and development centers. It also would make Jack, already a recognized business leader in his own right, appear to be simply a puppet of Yahoo! in China. To maintain Jack's credibility as a homegrown business leader, we had to make clear that we were still in charge.

"Porter, the way we announce this is critical. Tomorrow, when we go in there to discuss the announcement, we need you to be tough!" Jack instructed me.

The negotiations took on greater urgency on August 7, when the headline from Forbes.com hit everyone's in-box: "Yahoo! in Talks on Record China Investment." Someone had leaked the story, and the full details of the deal were in plain view. I immediately received a call from Mylene Mangalindan, a Bay Area–based correspondent for the *Wall Street Journal* who had been covering Alibaba's battle with eBay.

"Hi, Porter, I read the rumors. So where are you now?"

"Oh, I'm back here in the US for a personal trip," I replied. I could tell she didn't believe me.

"So is there any truth to this, Porter?"

I had never been formally trained as a PR man, let alone involved in a deal this size, and I hesitated. I finally gave her the company line that Yahoo!'s communications chief, Christine Castro, had provided me: "We don't comment on rumors and speculation."

"Oh, come on, Porter, everyone does it. Just let me know if there's any truth to this."

I clammed up and repeated my corporate line. "I'm sorry, we don't comment on rumors and speculation."

Frustrated, Mylene got off the phone, saying, "Okay, let me know if you change your mind."

I didn't know where the leak had come from, but I suspected the source was one of our investors, since the public revelation of our negotiations put additional pressure on Yahoo!. We soon heard that the report had thrown the Yahoo! China team into upheaval. The idea that Yahoo! China might be sold to Alibaba would be a huge loss of face for Zhou Hongyi.

The rumors also spurred eBay into action. eBay had likely assumed it was Alibaba's only suitor and its executives could take their time. Joe Tsai immediately received a call from eBay's head of corporate development, who was hoping to reignite partnership discussions. And we were told by Softbank's team that Meg Whitman was desperately trying to reach Masayoshi Son, Softbank's CEO, but he was ignoring her calls.

The next day I headed to Yahoo!'s Silicon Valley offices to join the partnership discussions and coordinate the announcement with Yahoo!'s PR team. Yahoo!'s COO, Dan Rosensweig, led the talks that day. Tall and boisterous, he was a dominant figure. "We'd be in the lead in China already if it wasn't for your government blocking us all these years!" he joked with Jack.

As we worked on the press release, Jack pulled me out of the meeting room to discuss the negotiating strategy.

"In a few minutes Jerry Yang is going to call to discuss how we position this. I want you to be very strong about how we need to phrase this as 'Alibaba Acquiring Yahoo! China' and not the other way around," he said. "Don't worry about me—I'm going to sit back and listen in. I'll jump in if I feel I need to."

With our good cop–bad cop strategy lined up, I jumped on the conference call. Ultimately we decided to describe the deal as a partnership and a combination of Yahoo! China and Alibaba. We left the press release vague enough that each side could call the deal whatever it wanted to when talking to its own investors. But we knew that same ambiguity also ensured there would be a race between Alibaba and Yahoo! to tell their version of events.

With the press release finished, one of the last remaining stumbling blocks to a deal was removed. Over lunch the next day Joe pulled out the contract's signature pages for Jack to sign so they could be attached to the body of the contract once the final details were hammered out. Jack signed the pages, and we started to talk about how to manage the announcement back in China. "You should fly directly to Beijing," Jack said. "We're going to have the announcement there. This is going to be big news."

Later that night I got a call from Joe as I packed my bags. "Porter, I'm sorry to say, but it looks like the deal is off. Yahoo! has added a last-minute demand to the contract. They are now insisting on calling the new combined business 'Alibaba-Yahoo!' That would create real problems for us in China. And not only that, I don't think we can do business with a partner who tries to sneak in such a big condition at the last minute."

The Yahoo! people apparently assumed we'd cave at the last minute.

"I was planning to fly back tomorrow to China," I said. "Should I just go ahead and do that, and tell Yahoo!'s PR team that you sent me back because the deal is off?"

"Yeah, good idea," Joe replied. "I'll see you back in China."

Later that night I got a call from Chris Castro, Yahoo!'s head of corporate communications. Chris asked: "Porter, when should we meet tomorrow to go over the new draft of the press release?"

"Oh, Jack and Joe told me that the deal is off. You hadn't heard that?" I asked. "So I'm flying out tomorrow morning."

Chris seemed surprised and concerned. "No, actually, I hadn't heard anything like that. Are you sure?"

"Yeah, I'm flying back tomorrow. It's too bad the deal didn't work out, as I would have liked to work with you."

The next day, I got on the plane and settled in for the long flight to Shanghai. I admired Jack and Joe for standing up to Yahoo! on principle. I probably wouldn't have had the conviction to turn down a $1 billion cash offer. But I also felt a twinge of regret. The Yahoo! deal would have put us in the global spotlight and ensured that Alibaba had enough in the coffers to sustain eBay's $100 million assault on us.

Upon touching down in Shanghai, I picked up my bags and got in a taxi. The familiar gray skies hovering over the countryside told me I was back to life as usual.

I turned on my phone and it began to ring almost immediately. It was Jack.

"Hey, Jack, what's up? I just touched down in Shanghai."

Jack's voice had an excited and urgent tone. "Get on the next flight you can to Beijing. Yahoo!'s given in on the final point—the deal is back on! We're announcing it the day after tomorrow."

THE DEAL HEARD 'ROUND THE WORLD

JOURNALISTS PACED AROUND THE LOBBY OF BEI-
jing's China World Hotel, hoping to grab a stray Alibaba or
Yahoo! executive to mine for advance information. The deal
was not yet officially public, but that hadn't stopped a flood
of leaks that set Chinese and foreign journalists alike into a
frenzy. Behind closed doors, in an unmarked meeting room, we
gathered a team of about 12 Alibaba and Yahoo! executives
to work out the logistics of our announcement. With the com-
motion outside, all pretense of the meeting's being secret was
dropped—which at least lightened the mood in the room.

"This is insanity," Dan Rosensweig, Yahoo!'s COO, joked.
"It's a circus out there. There is nothing left to announce!"

This was the first time we had met our Yahoo! counterparts in Asia, so we took a few moments to introduce the two
teams. Rose Tsou was a sharp managing director of Yahoo!
Taiwan with a dry sense of humor and a no-nonsense approach
to getting things done. Allan Kwan was the smart and friendly
Hong Kong–based regional head of Yahoo!'s operations. And

Lu Qi, the head of Yahoo!'s global search technology, would be our main partner for developing and improving Yahoo! China's search engine. We seemed to have a good common language, and it seemed the basis for a good partnership.

Noticeably absent from the meeting was Zhou Hongyi, the head of Yahoo! China. Even though Jack and Zhou had once been friends, some people were concerned about Zhou's reaction to the deal. "Our relationship with the Yahoo! China team has gotten so bad that Zhou Hongyi has stopped hiring managers who speak English," a member of Yahoo!'s California PR team told me. "He's hardly willing to talk to us anymore."

But integrating Yahoo! China into our own operations was going to be the key to a successful partnership. To help ease the process Yahoo! US had flown a human relations specialist out to Beijing, and he seemed especially concerned about the challenge of bringing the two teams together. We agreed that Jack's first step, immediately after the press conference, would be to address the Yahoo! China managers.

Finally it was time. On August 11, we arrived at the large conference hall to find a room packed with media from around the world. Journalists filled the chairs and stood along the walls to record this historic milestone for China's Internet. It was clear that this was more than just an announcement. It was Alibaba's coming out party.

Dan Rosensweig sat on stage with Jack and several Alibaba executives. "This is Yahoo! getting much bigger in China. We look at this as an opportunity to get much bigger, much faster, working with a great management team," Dan said. When Jack took the stage and laid out the vision for the new partnership, he couldn't resist a small jab at eBay, saying, "Thank you,

Meg Whitman. Thank you for making all of this possible." To mark the moment a loud *pop* sounded, and confetti streamed through the air, drifting onto the shoulders of Dan and Jack, who beamed as cameras flashed, capturing the moment for newspapers around the world.

After the press conference I was swarmed by foreign media. I had courted them for years; now they were finally chasing us. With microphones and tape recorders stuck into my face, I could sense that Alibaba was on an entirely new level. Aware my comments would be read back in Silicon Valley, I took my own opportunity for a mischievous swipe at my friends back at eBay: "This is really probably the knockout blow for eBay in China. This is going to make it hard for eBay to win in Asia. It totally reshapes the landscape for auctions in Asia." eBay's response was instantaneous: "It's business as usual for us," the eBay representative Hani Durzy told the Associated Press. "We will maintain our leading position in China," Liu Wei, eBay China's representative, told the *New York Times*. But despite the facade of confidence, we knew that eBay must have been concerned.

Later in the afternoon it was time for Jack to address Yahoo! China's senior management team. From our perspective it was an exciting moment, like welcoming new members to a family. To be sure, there would be moments of awkwardness. But one of Jack's finest assets was his ability to bring people together. So I was surprised when Brian Wong, who'd attended the meeting, reported to me that it hadn't gone well.

"It was really strange," Brian said. "Zhou Hongyi was there and had a really distraught look on his face. Just to be polite, Jack invited him on stage to talk to the team. Zhou's message to them was, 'I'm going to be leaving to start my own new venture. And if any of you are interested, you are welcome to join me.' He seems really bitter about this deal." Zhou Hongyi's call for Yahoo! China employees to abandon ship was the first real sign that we might have been sold a lemon. Even with Jack's strong leadership skills, integrating Yahoo! China's disgruntled team was clearly going to be harder than we'd thought.

During the next few weeks it became clear that the Yahoo! deal marked not only Alibaba's global coming out party but also its loss of innocence. For six years we'd been the scrappy underdog, a favorite of media and industry watchers who liked the idea that a company led by an English teacher was taking on the giants. But with a billion dollars flowing in and a major global partner, real money was now at stake. We were playing on a new level, and consequently the scale of attacks on us was growing too.

The first sign was a phone call I received from a journalist at the *Hollywood Reporter,* the day after our announcement with Yahoo!.

"I just received a strange fax I'd like to ask you about," he said. "It includes US congressional testimony from the International Anti-Counterfeiting Coalition earlier this year. They are claiming that Alibaba is the world's largest trading hub for counterfeit goods."

I immediately suspected eBay was behind the fax, based on the attack line Meg had recently used at eBay's annual shareholder meeting. Although it smacked of the pot's calling the kettle black, it seemed that eBay was weaving into its narrative the message that Alibaba was a clearinghouse for counterfeit goods. As a Chinese company Alibaba was an easy target for eBay and its political allies in Washington, perhaps even an easy way to deflect to us criticism of counterfeits on eBay.

"Interesting. Who sent the fax?" I asked.

"It didn't say. It was sent to me anonymously. There were no contact details. But I heard a number of other journalists also received it."

Someone was trying to smear us. Could it be that, if eBay couldn't buy us, it was going to do anything within its power to interfere with our Yahoo! deal? When Henry Gomez told me, "There is always a way of getting the word out," was this what he had in mind? I couldn't be 100 percent sure that eBay was behind it, but I realized that things might get really ugly really fast.

I told the reporter, "Well, we have the exact same policy as eBay, based on the same legal standard. If we are notified by a brand owner that one of our sellers has infringed on their intellectual property, we will investigate and take down the listing where appropriate."

The response seemed to satisfy the *Hollywood Reporter*, but responding to the crisis had taken up my entire morning, so I was late getting to Hangzhou for our all-hands staff meeting, which was being held at Hangzhou's Great Hall of the People. When I finally arrived, thousands of smiling and laughing Alibaba staff members, all dressed in white shirts emblazoned with the logos of both Alibaba and Yahoo!, were streaming out of the venue. Clearly the news had gone over better with the Alibaba team than with their Yahoo! counterparts in Beijing.

As people filed out of the auditorium, I found Dan Rosensweig next to the stage. "So what was your impression of the Alibaba team?" I asked, expecting him to be as effusive as I was feeling.

"It's very young," he said. "We're going to have to do a lot of training and bring in some expertise from the US." I was slightly offended, not to mention reminded of the way our own Hong Kong expats had reacted to meeting the Alibaba team for the first time. It was a good reminder of why we'd made sure to maintain management control in our deal, to avoid too much oversight from the Yahoo! US team's prying eyes. But I kept my mouth shut.

Just then Jack walked over.

"Hey, Jack, nice job today," Dan said. "If this partnership goes well, maybe someday we'll go ahead and buy the rest of Alibaba."

Jack laughed. "Well, I think someday, if you play your cards right, maybe Alibaba will buy Yahoo!." I looked at Jack and realized that he was only half joking.

"Ha, I don't think so," Dan replied. Clearly he thought Jack's boast was cute but preposterous. "Last I checked, Yahoo! was worth $40 billion and Alibaba was worth $4 billion. You've got a long way to go."

With the deal announced, it was time to turn our attention to the next big media frenzy, Alibaba's annual West Lake Summit. Jack had started the event back in 2001, at the depths of the Internet winter, when he brought together the CEOs of five of China's leading Internet companies. Over time the summit came to be regarded as a sort of Davos for China's Internet industry, and this year's event would have a very special keynote speaker—former US president Bill Clinton.

The introduction to Bill Clinton had come through Marcy Simon, who had her own small PR firm which counted the Clinton Foundation as one of her clients. Marcy had approached me at a conference I'd attended with Jack. She'd seen Jack speak a couple of times, had grown into a fan, and wanted to see if she could work for us. Given her background—she had worked for Bill Gates as well—she certainly seemed like someone who could help with our PR efforts in the US, so we retained her as a consultant. Not long after she began working on our PR campaigns, she introduced us to Bill Clinton's staff.

Having a former US president speak at our event was quite a source of pride for Alibaba. Clinton was broadly popular and one of the few Westerners who could argue credibly to a Chinese audience about the need to open China's Internet. When his keynote appearance was announced, China's blogosphere lit up with excitement.

But several weeks before the event eBay tried to get Clinton to cancel. When I approached Joe Tsai with a small question, he responded sharply, "I can't deal with this right now—I'm trying to make sure Clinton still speaks at our event. eBay is trying to get him not to speak." I was shocked and worried. If Clinton pulled out, it would be a devastating blow to Alibaba's reputation in China and a major loss of face for Jack. Surely eBay knew this, and if it succeeded, Alibaba would suffer serious damage while we were still in the process of closing our deal with Yahoo!.

The picture grew even clearer when I was forwarded a PowerPoint presentation that eBay's general counsel had sent to Clinton's assistant, Doug Band. On it were screenshots from Alibaba's website showing postings for illicit items such as AK-47s, uranium, and counterfeit goods. While the vast majority of the products posted on Alibaba were legitimate, it was impossible for Alibaba to screen out all the bad actors. The website policy—and applicable laws—stated that members were responsible for their postings. A marketplace operator like Alibaba was simply responsible for taking down illegal postings when made aware of them. But it was clear that some illegal listings had made it onto the site. The big question was how Clinton's team would react.

In addition to the email from eBay's general counsel, I heard from Marcy that eBay's founder, Pierre Omidiyar, a billionaire donor to Clinton's foundation, had called Clinton and pleaded with him not to attend our West Lake Summit. "In fact, he made two calls," Marcy said. It was a full-court press.

I found it ironic that, just a few weeks earlier, eBay was desperately trying to invest in Alibaba but was now doing everything within its power to smear us. Fortunately eBay failed to land its blows and Marcy informed us that Clinton would still attend the summit, despite eBay's protests. "I explained to Clinton, it's just because eBay is competing with Alibaba," she told me.

A few weeks later Clinton's plane touched down in Hangzhou. The city had worked hard to provide a suitable welcome. As the motorcade rolled to the entrance of the Grand Hyatt, fountains on the West Lake swayed to orchestral music while Chinese tourists lined the hotel perimeter, hoping to get a glimpse of the former president. The city's pride was still recovering from comments made by the last US president to visit Hangzhou—Richard Nixon—who reportedly had remarked, "Beautiful lake, ugly city." Local officials were determined not to let that happen this time.

After Clinton strolled through the hotel lobby and went up to the presidential suite, Jack approached me with an urgent request. "Porter, I've never asked you to write a speech for me. But this is the one time I think I need your help. Can you write the introduction for me to introduce Bill Clinton?" Sure, I said. This time *was* different. So I headed to my hotel room to work on Jack's opening comments.

As I was writing Jack's speech, Marcy pulled Jack aside and told him that he and Joe were invited up to Clinton's suite to chat and get to know each other. It was the night before Jack's birthday, and Marcy surprised him with a birthday cake, which they shared with Clinton. As Marcy would tell me later, Clinton joked with Jack about eBay's antics leading up to the summit, saying with a laugh, "Boy, those eBay folks sure are mad at you." Luckily Clinton and Jack hit it off, setting the tone for what we assumed would be a successful summit.

Until the next day, when I woke up to a press release issued by Reporters Without Borders and Human Rights in China: "Clinton Urged to Raise Shi Tao Case at China Internet Summit." I read further to learn that Reporters Without Borders was reporting that Yahoo! had provided a journalist's email information to the Chinese government which had then sentenced the Beijing reporter to ten years in prison for "leaking state secrets" to foreign media. All the journalist, Shi Tao, had done was leak a Communist Party directive to Chinese journalists that they should not report on the upcoming fifteenth anniversary of the Tiananmen Square massacre. When Shi Tao sent the document to foreign journalists, he had assumed that by using Yahoo! China, rather than a local email provider, he would be able to maintain his anonymity. But when the Chinese government asked for the user information, Yahoo!'s legal team handed it over, exposing Shi Tao as the source.

Suddenly it was obvious that when we acquired Yahoo! China, we had acquired a political time bomb. As we headed into a radio interview, I briefed Jack on the issue—it was the first he'd heard about it. When I spoke to Mary Osako, a member of Yahoo!'s communications team, she told me that Yahoo! would be canceling Jerry Yang's appearance at the press conference that was supposed to follow Jerry's planned fireside chat with Jack at the summit. "The only thing the foreign media are going to want to talk about is the Shi Tao case," she told me.

The conference began without a hitch. We had persuaded the local Hangzhou television station to broadcast Bill Clinton's speech live, a rarity in China. When Clinton took the stage, he made no mention of the Shi Tao case. Instead he argued persuasively, "Whatever political system a country has, the Internet has the potential to put power through information and communication in the hands of ordinary people. And I think on balance that has to be a good thing, anywhere in the world."

Then Jerry and Jack took the stage for their fireside chat. It was the first time Jack and Jerry, together in the same room, laid out their common vision for the partnership. They discussed how they'd first met in Beijing, traveled to the Great Wall together, and ultimately crossed paths again at Pebble Beach in the fateful meeting that had led to the partnership. A Q&A session followed the fireside chat. Peter Goodman of the *Washington Post* stood up to ask the last question and addressed the controversy:

"Mr. Yang, your company was founded at a time when Internet companies were marketing themselves to consumers and to shareholders and the public as not merely business propositions but almost forces for liberation, for freedom of information, free flow of information, freedom of expression. There are now people saying that your company is effectively a tool of the Chinese government, that you've become a force for repression. How does that make you feel personally? And what can you tell us about your company's role in the Shi Tao case?"[1]

The room was filled with silence as Jerry Yang ruminated over the question. When he finally answered, he fumbled through a lengthy explanation:

"We don't know what they want that information for, we're not told what they look for. If they give us the proper documentation and court orders, we give them things that satisfy both our privacy and the local rules. I do not like the outcome of what happens with these things."[2]

From a PR perspective Jerry was caught between the Chinese government and US politicians. Any comment from him, however deft, would likely dominate the headlines the next day. But his wishy-washy answer left the impression that even Yahoo!'s cofounder didn't believe its actions in China were justified. In my opinion Yahoo! could have reasonably argued that the net effect of Western Internet companies in China was to create a more open society there. But instead Jerry tried to straddle the fence, and to critics in the West he appeared to lack a moral center.

For his part Jack gained applause from the mostly local crowd: "As a business, if you cannot change the law, follow the law. Respect the local government. We're not interested in politics. We're focused on e-commerce." That response, too, would never satisfy all the Western critics. But at least it seemed born of clarity and conviction, of Jack's own deepest beliefs.

When the *Washington Post* came out the next day, on September 11, the headline read: "Yahoo Says It Gave China Internet Data." Neither Yahoo! nor Alibaba came across well in the article, and even Clinton was drawn into the controversy, with Goodman reporting, "Clinton did not mention the Shi case in his speech. As he was leaving the hall, the former president declined to answer a question about the case before melting into a thicket of Chinese security and Secret Service officers." Marcy later told me that Clinton had been blindsided by the issue and was furious at his staff for not properly briefing him. But all was not lost. "At least the president liked Jack," Doug Band, Clinton's assistant, told me later.

As we worked to close our deal with Yahoo!, the Shi Tao case continued to hang over us. Until this point Alibaba had been fortunate to operate in the politically neutral domain of e-commerce. But in acquiring Yahoo! China, we were stepping into a new domain, operating a portal that included news, information, and communication services, such as chat and email. It was the first controversy to drive a wedge between Yahoo! and Alibaba, but I was betting it wouldn't be the last.

More troubling to me was that I had to think about my own role in a company that now operated a general portal that was beholden to China's laws concerning privacy and censorship. As an American I had a luxury that my local colleagues did not—I could choose whether to work within the constraints of China's laws. I had started my career by teaching leadership workshops in Washington, DC, that promoted democracy to high school students and encouraged them to learn about America's democratic processes. By staying with Alibaba was I somehow betraying the very values I had so fervently espoused?

But I didn't dwell on this thought for long, as I could see the benefits that the Internet was bringing to China every day. Compared to my student days in Beijing in 1994, when government minders opened my mail and even a fax machine had to be registered with the government, China had become a much more open society. Sure, it was not a Western-style representative democracy. But individual liberties were expanding every day. It was just a matter of time, I thought, before the Internet, a Trojan horse, forced China to open to an even greater extent. Besides, I figured, widespread adoption of e-commerce in China meant one thing—the government could never simply pull the plug on the Internet in China. If the government censored blogs or media content, the local population would be irritated. But if the government pulled the plug on millions of shop owners who depended on the Internet for their livelihoods, people would take to the streets.

Of course, executives of American companies faced the same moral choice when deciding whether to operate within China. A year earlier, at our meeting with the Google executives, I had admired Sergey Brin's efforts to find a way to operate in China without compromising the company's values. At that time, Google decided that the benefit to the Chinese of a more open Internet was in keeping with its famous corporate principle, "Don't be evil." But Google's leaders had also promised that if the compromises grew to be too much, they would pull out of the China market (ultimately this is precisely what they did). Yahoo! had offered no such assurance. Its message was simply that it wanted to profit from the China market.

In a way I was relieved that this news had broken before we closed the deal. My biggest fear was that Alibaba would somehow be dragged into the morass with Yahoo! and, as a Chinese company, be seen as the enemy. I had seen a young idealistic team survive and thrive *despite* government restrictions on the Internet, not *because* of them. If the same thing happened after the deal was done, Alibaba would be an easy target. But as it turned out, Yahoo!'s fumbling of the communication left it alone in the crosshairs. Not long after the Shi Tao revelation, Yahoo! would be called to Congress to testify about its actions in China.

By the end of the West Lake Summit, the Alibaba-Yahoo! coming out party had been far overshadowed by the Shi Tao case, at least in the Western media. However, China's censorship regime prevented local media from covering the controversy, so the Chinese public never heard about it. But while the issue was not on the radar of the general public, and our customers in China, we could only assume that it was on the radar of Chinese government officials. So we still had to tread carefully to ensure that the government would approve the deal.

To this end I went with Jack to meet with Wang Guoping, the local Communist Party secretary. I'd met Wang a few times before, and he always surprised me by defying the stereotype of a boring Communist bureaucrat who spoke only in party platitudes. Chubby and bespectacled, Wang Guoping was outspoken, funny, and even brash. He was a giant version of our COO Liqi and more closely resembled Hangzhou's results-oriented local entrepreneurs than Beijing's bureaucrats. He was regarded as holding the real power in Hangzhou, more so than the feeble mayor, Mao Linsheng, despite the difference in their titles. Secretary Wang was as much a capitalist as any Communist Party secretary could be, and it was a good thing for Hangzhou, as it was for Alibaba.

The meeting took place in a quiet cluster of teahouses on the lush grounds around the West Lake. When I arrived, Jack and Wang Guoping were already sitting together, chatting over tea, as is typical protocol for such an event. Lining Jack's side of the room, in order of rank, was Alibaba's senior management team. Lining Wang Guoping's side, in order of rank, were local government officials. With every word Wang spoke, the officials went through the customary motions of taking notes.

Our main goal for the meeting was to impress upon the local leaders the significance and global impact of the deal. There were many ways businesses sought to please the local government in China—some clean and some not—and we had always done the right thing in the belief that the best way to gain government support was to show that you were attracting business, attention, and investment to the city. To this end, before meeting with Wang Guoping, Jack had called me and asked me to print out the full set of articles the West Lake Summit had generated in the Western media about the event. The result was a printout of Alibaba news clippings that ran for several hundred pages. While many of the reports discussed the Shi Tao controversy, I'd made sure they were at the bottom of the stack and hoped Wang wouldn't read that far.

After exchanging small talk with Wang Guoping, Jack motioned for me to hand over the media clippings and said, "Porter, tell Secretary Wang about the international media coverage."

"The deal has been in the headlines all around the world," I said. "All of the leading media have been reporting on it. I think a lot of people are seeing Hangzhou as the center for e-commerce in China."

Wang Guoping nodded in approval. Our West Lake Summit had propelled his city into the global spotlight. Then Wang had a question:

"But Manager Ma, one thing I'm still a little confused about is, for once and for all, can you tell me: Did Alibaba acquire Yahoo! or did Yahoo! acquire Alibaba?"

Wang Guoping wasn't the only one with this question in China. Following our announcement, the headlines had repeatedly asked, "Who acquired whom?," sending our local PR team into crisis mode to argue our case to the local media. The confusion made clear to me why Jack had been so insistent upon rejecting Yahoo!'s request to rename our company "Alibaba-Yahoo!." Doing so would have only confused the market and put our efforts in China at risk.

Jack answered confidently, "Alibaba is buying Yahoo! China, and we have full management control of the company. And there are a few important things I need to share with you. Number one, Alibaba's headquarters will stay here in Hangzhou. Number two, we have a provision in the contract that, no matter what, a member of Alibaba's board will have to be from China. And finally Yahoo! is putting $1 billion into the company. It's going to really create a great number of jobs here in Hangzhou and help with the mission of making sure Hangzhou becomes China's Silicon Valley."

Wang Guoping nodded and smiled as he mulled it over. "Good. Good." Jack and Wang chatted a little more, and then Secretary Wang concluded the meeting with the words we'd hoped to hear as his assistants transcribed his comments: "I want to say that the Hangzhou government totally supports this special 'Alibaba merger model.' Congratulations to Jack Ma and Alibaba!"

With the local government providing its support, we had cleared an important hurdle. But we knew that greater challenges lay ahead.

THE CHINA SEARCH WARS

ON OCTOBER 25, 2005, TEN ROCKY WEEKS AFTER announcing our deal with Yahoo!, we became the legal guardian of our new baby—Yahoo! China. Two weeks later we were back in Beijing at a press conference to announce the reintroduction of Yahoo! China to the national Chinese media. In typical Alibaba form our marketing machine had packed the room with journalists curious to see what we had to unveil.

Before the press conference Jack laid out his strategy—and it was straight out of the playbook from our battle with eBay. "I want to position this as a battle between Yahoo! China and Baidu," Jack told me. If we could engage Baidu, the local search engine leader, in a war of words, we could drive traffic to Yahoo! China's search engine.

Although Baidu had a stronger understanding of the local market than eBay did, Baidu in many ways seemed an easier opponent to defeat. Founded by Robin Li, a soft-spoken entrepreneur who'd studied and worked in the US in the 1990s, Baidu had simply followed the Google script in China. Each time Google introduced a new function, Baidu quickly followed suit, offering a similar feature on its own website. Its home page was practically identical to Google's; Baidu had become the market leader in China by simply pursuing a "fast-follower" strategy: mimicking the Google US model and providing it locally before Google had a chance to bring each feature to the local market. As a competitor Robin Li seemed better at imitation than innovation, and we thought he'd be no match for our more creative team. In the race for the China market Baidu was only a couple strides ahead, with a 37 percent market share of searches, compared to a 32 percent market share for Yahoo! China, and a 19 percent share for Google. Surely we could catch up to Baidu in a few short months.

We had plenty of reasons to be confident. Against all odds we'd survived a war with America's B2B giants and Alibaba had emerged as the world's largest B2B marketplace. And despite all the skepticism from outside (and sometimes within) Taobao had pulled ahead in our battle with eBay in China. I'd learned to suspend all doubts and accept that, if Jack said it was possible, it must be possible. He'd never failed us before. So, as Jack stood on the stage of the press conference for the grand unveiling of Yahoo! China, I was feeling good about our prospects.

"From now on in China, *Yahoo!* means *search* and *search* means *Yahoo!*," Jack proclaimed. "In six months Yahoo! China has to be the leader in the China market, otherwise the game will be over." Jack; John Wu, Alibaba's chief technology officer; and the Yahoo! China team gathered around a mock button on the stage. Pressing the button revealed the new Yahoo! home page on the screen behind them—a stark white page with nothing but the Yahoo! China logo and a search bar in the middle. Gone were the flashing images, links, directory, news, and information found on the previous version of Yahoo! China. The site was no longer a general portal—it was a pure search engine. And the race with Baidu and Google was on.

As 2005 became 2006, the Alibaba marketing machine was in overdrive, promoting Yahoo! China in a major rebranding effort. Our website may have been dry and functional. But the marketing surrounding it was exciting and designed to capture the imagination of China's Internet users. We sponsored flashy Chinese music awards celebrations with the latest pop stars and paid $1 million to each of three famous film directors to produce television commercials for Yahoo! China. Whereas we had once depended on our zero budget marketing efforts, which simply relied on great user experience and word of mouth, now we were spending millions of dollars to make our big splash.

Yet for all the buzz the traffic data were a source of concern. Since we had stripped the Yahoo! China site of its features and reintroduced it as a straightforward search portal, its traffic had dropped off a cliff, and our market share was slipping quickly. Rather than wait out the storm and see if traffic on the newly simplified home page would stabilize as the search engine improved, Jack abruptly took the Yahoo! China home page back to its original look. But when website traffic didn't bounce back, it became clear that our shifting strategies had killed off a portion of our customer base. Worse, we had confused the market, appearing erratic as we veered back and forth. To China's Internet users, the quick reversal smacked of desperation, and the media were quick to pounce on Alibaba for appearing rudderless and abandoning Yahoo! China's new emphasis on search.

As our strategy careened out of control, I began to wonder whether Jack's considerable management skills would translate to running a search engine. After managing our Google campaign and visiting the Googleplex as a customer, I had become both a student and an admirer of Google's. I'd learned that Google's biggest key to success was its singular focus on first building the best search technology in the world. Google had resisted all distractions, and over time Internet users had rewarded it by migrating to Google's superior interface and search technology. With this in mind I handed Jack a copy of John Battelle's in-depth book about Google, *The Search*. "Jack, this is a great book about how Google became so successful," I said. "Now that we've got Yahoo! China, you might want to take a look. It's really good."

Jack turned the book away. "Someone once tried to give me a book about eBay," he said, "but I didn't want to read it. I wanted to make sure we didn't just copy their approach. You should give that to somebody else. I don't want to get too focused on what they did because it may bias me to follow Google's approach."

While I admired Jack's insistence upon innovating in his own way, it also concerned me. We didn't need to *copy* Google. But we could at least *learn* from them. Jack was a marketing person who knew how to mobilize millions of people to join a community to trade products online. But a search engine was a totally different animal. Searching is not a community activity. The only relationship was between the user and the search engine. People didn't go on Baidu or Google to make friends and chat; they went to find other websites and move on.

By the time our 2006 strategy meeting arrived, tensions within Yahoo! China were beginning to bubble up. Some of the Yahoo! China managers had already left the company to join Zhou Hongyi in his new venture. And those remaining had little reason to believe that Jack's vision for a search engine in China would become a reality. Unlike those of us coming from the Alibaba side, the Yahoo! China team had not weathered storms or defeated Internet giants together. They largely saw Jack as most outsiders did—fascinating but unpredictable. And Jack's management of the Yahoo! China strategy had done little to persuade them otherwise.

During the strategy meeting members of Yahoo! China's technical team got up to present their ideas for moving the search engine's strategy forward. They discussed the importance of having the right technology in place and the best algorithms for searches. I could see Jack's eyes glaze over. He didn't have time or interest in these technical details. To him technology was secondary to the user experience. And he wasn't shy about it. "People can't tell the difference between one search engine or another," he argued. "From the user perspective they're all the same. The most important thing is our marketing strategy." The team was quiet, obviously not comfortable contradicting their new boss. But with this one comment I realized how fundamentally Jack misunderstood search engines. And my guess was that, unless something changed his mind soon, Yahoo! China would be doomed.

As we executed our poorly defined strategy, Yahoo! China's performance continued to suffer. Making matters worse, we were receiving phone calls from headhunters claiming to be recruiting staff for Zhou's new venture, Qihoo.com. Internally, we believed this to be an effort by Qihoo to damage our team's morale. We made our suspicions public and were quickly sued by Zhou Hongyi on defamation charges.

Meanwhile, Qihoo's new technology began to get a surprising level of traction, as China's Internet users downloaded its 360Safe antivirus toolbar and installed it on their computers.

Hidden in the toolbar was a feature that blocked Yahoo! China services from the user's computer, labeling our services as malware. As the number of downloads increased, Yahoo! China's website traffic continued to taper off.

Zhou Hongyi aired his grievances against Alibaba to the Chinese media and Jack was quick to publicly respond. Over time the public volleys between the two companies grew into an ugly dogfight that made neither party look good. It was a huge distraction, and it meant that 2006 would be about fighting Qihoo, not Baidu. By engaging us in a war of words, Zhou Hongyi had taken a page out of our playbook and managed to get under Jack Ma's skin. As Yahoo! China's audience continued to disappear, Jack started to do exactly what he had faulted Meg Whitman for back in the eBay days—he took it too personally. To be sure, Qihoo's actions were affecting Yahoo! China's performance. But Jack seemed to be increasingly obsessed with Zhou Hongyi himself, and rather than focusing on building Yahoo! China's search capabilities into a world-class technology, Jack poured his energy into fighting back. To this end we brought— and immediately got bogged down in—a lawsuit against Qihoo alleging unfair competition. Although we ultimately won the suit, which helped restore some of our team's pride, the lawsuit had no material effect on Yahoo! China, and Qihoo was required to pay only RMB 30,000 (about $4,000) in damages. As 2006 came to an end, for the first time Alibaba's senior managers were beginning to ask whether Jack was losing his magic touch. "Jack has lost his way with the Yahoo! strategy," a senior manager confided in me. I couldn't help but agree.

Luckily things were looking much brighter on the other side of our company.

FREE IS NOT A
BUSINESS MODEL

WHILE WE WERE FAILING AT BECOMING THE MOST popular search engine in China, there was one field where no one could beat us—marketplaces. On the B2B front Alibaba .com's revenue growth continued to shoot toward the stars. And on the consumer front Taobao was growing 50 percent faster than eBay, at last surpassing our US counterpart on the all-important GMV (gross merchandise volume) metric.

After the Yahoo! China deal was announced, Henry Gomez of eBay had told *Fortune* magazine, "Jack Ma's strategy is to drive his competitors crazy. Now he's likely to drive Yahoo crazy as well." Gomez was right on both counts. Our cowboy style and shifting strategies were creating friction with our new US partner. But Taobao's relentless growth was driving eBay crazy as well. And we weren't done yet.

The week that Yahoo!'s $1 billion hit Alibaba's bank account coincided with eBay's quarterly earnings announcement. With our war chest fully funded, we had the confidence to deliver the knockout blow. Just as eBay prepared to release its earnings report, we issued a press release targeting the US media and eBay's investors. The announcement was a direct strike at eBay:

Taobao.com to Be Free of Charge
for Three More Years
China's Leading Consumer Auction Site to
Invest US $120 million in China Market to Grow
e-Commerce and Create One Million Jobs

Alibaba.com announced today that its Taobao.com Chinese-language consumer auction site will remain free for buyers and sellers for three more years. . . . In addition, Alibaba.com will invest US$120 million to further grow Taobao.com's trusted e-commerce marketplace with the goal of creating one million jobs for entrepreneurs in China.

"Taobao.com is committed to fostering the development of e-commerce in China while building China's largest and most trusted online consumer marketplace," said Alibaba.com CEO Jack Ma. . . .

Since its 2003 launch, Taobao.com has pioneered an e-commerce model truly tailored for the China consumer. Being free has allowed Taobao.com to grow its user base while encouraging [the] online community as the company listens to customers to understand the unique needs of buyers and sellers in China.

The message appealed to our audiences on several levels. First, it sent a message to eBay's investors that we were serious about keeping our services free, ensuring that eBay would face pricing pressure for the next several years. It also gave our customers in China confidence that if they stuck with Taobao for another three years, they could continue to grow their businesses before having to cough up fees. And then we added the kicker:

A Call to eBay

In addition to its pledge to make Taobao free until October 2008, Taobao.com called on eBay to join Taobao in making its services free for Chinese users. "We call on eBay to do what's right for this phase of China's e-commerce development and make your services free for buyers and sellers in China," said Jack Ma. . . . "Cutting prices is not enough—it's time to make your services free and affordable for all of China's entrepreneurs and consumers."

It was a bold taunt, designed to provoke a reaction. Although we didn't expect eBay to respond, it would at least make it harder for Meg Whitman to cut eBay's prices without losing face in China. Finally, just to show we weren't entirely crazy, we included in the press release the rationale for our strategy to demonstrate that, yes, we did have a long-term plan to charge for our services:

The Alibaba Precedent—First Free, Then Profitable

"Free is the right business model for China's current conditions," said Jack Ma. "But Taobao.com is a business, and like any serious business we have a solid plan for profitability. With Alibaba and Taobao, our theory has always been, only after our members make money using our marketplaces should we make money." Alibaba.com's business-to-business marketplaces, Alibaba International and Alibaba China,

started free for members and then matured into highly profitable businesses, generating US$68 million in cash revenues in
2004 with revenue growth doubling year-on-year.

The reaction from Wall Street was instantaneous—eBay's
stock dropped 6 percent. In a knee-jerk reaction Henry Gomez
issued a public response from eBay:

Statement from eBay Regarding
Taobao's Pricing Challenge

"Free" is not a business model. It speaks volumes about the
strength of eBay's business in China that Taobao today announced that it is unable to charge for its products for the next
three years.

We're very proud that eBay is creating a sustainable business in China, while providing Chinese consumers and entrepreneurs with the safest, most professional, and most exciting
global trading environment available today.

eBay
Henry Gomez
Hani Durzy

We couldn't help but chuckle when we saw that. We'd officially brought eBay down to our level. Our public call to eBay
may have been appropriate for a scrappy David who was taking
a swing at a Goliath. But we felt that what seemed such an emotional response from the world's largest e-commerce company
made it look weak and foolish, and eBay was promptly criticized in the media and blogosphere.

To coincide with our announcement we'd invited a number of local reporters to a small press conference in our office, where we handed out eBay's statement along with our own. I smiled to myself about what we were doing.

Jack explained to the reporters why Taobao was on track to win the race for consumers in China. "The business model for charging is already proven in the States. You don't have to prove the model, you have to prove how big the market is. You have to prove that you can create value in this market, but they just did not listen. *Free* is still a good word for C2C [consumer to consumer] because it's so premature in this market. Only 8 percent of Internet users here have tried online shopping. So among one hundred people, 92 people have not tried it."

"Do you think eBay's time is over?" Jack was asked.

"Almost over. It's too late for them. Unless they do something really meaningful. Business is fun, competition is fun, but don't take it too seriously," Jack continued. "They took it too seriously in China, for competition. Not on creating real value for the Chinese market and Chinese consumers. That's the main reason they'll lose. Just watch—soon we'll be the only ones left. eBay's days are numbered."

Having lured eBay from its lair, we spent the next few months upping the pressure on eBay, showing that eBay's argument was not logical. If "free is not a business model," we wondered to all who would listen, then why was its newly acquired Skype service free? Why was PayPal free? And why was Craigslist, in which eBay owned a stake, free?

As we continued our taunts, public opinion began to move in our favor. eBay was in trouble, and the media and analysts knew it. In late 2005 eBay's market share slipped to 34 percent, compared to Taobao's 57 percent. Seeing its market slipping away, eBay finally decided to eliminate transaction fees on its China websites. On January 19, 2006, as news broke that eBay was eliminating fees in China, its stock went into freefall. Rather than embracing the move, foreign and local publications responded by mocking eBay, with headlines like "eBay Decides 'Free' Is a Business Model." It was clear that eBay had lost the confidence of investors, as its stock dropped nearly 50 percent during the next six months. eBay was in serious trouble.

As eBay China drifted into irrelevance, Jack addressed Taobao's employees at a team event to celebrate Taobao's three-year anniversary. Jack reminded the team to focus on the big picture:

> Taobao is not only a hot topic in China, it is also a hot topic in the US. Everyone is wondering how long the competition with eBay will last and when will eBay retreat. But I want everyone to keep things in perspective. In the past our competition with eBay was fierce, but I want everyone to keep in mind one proverb: "If we have no enemies in our heart, we will be invincible to the world." We should not be ruthless to our enemies.
>
> The thing I'm most proud of about Taobao is that we are not only doing a great job for ourselves but also providing employment opportunities to millions of people. So I hope in the next three years we will not consider competition the main priority. Competition has become the second or third priority. The most important thing is to continue increasing Taobao's transaction volume and user base. It's not about defeating someone. It's about how large we can grow the market.

It was an important reminder to the team. Yes, we'd had a number of corporate battles with eBay. But more important than any of the marketing or PR tactics was that we were building a real infrastructure for consumer commerce in China. Building a marketplace that truly empowered entrepreneurs was what had gotten us this far. And if we were to continue to succeed, we couldn't lose sight of this purpose.

During the next several months the volume of eBay's marketing and PR campaigns fell to a whisper in China, and we began to hear rumors that its executives were looking for a face-saving way to exit the market. So we weren't surprised when, at the end of 2006, eBay announced that it was shutting down its China website and handing its China operations over to a new joint venture partner, Tom Online. Although it was backed by the Hong Kong billionaire Li Ka-shing, Tom Online was mostly a nonfactor in the China market.

The announcement came during the Christmas season, no doubt timed to hit in the midst of a slow news cycle with journalists more focused on holidays than the latest tech news from China. eBay's spin on the announcement was that it was doubling down in China and backing a local partner, in the same way that Yahoo! had done with us. But the eBay-Tom partnership was widely recognized for what it was—a de facto withdrawal from the China market. Given that Tom Online only had to put up $20 million for a 51 percent stake in their newly formed joint venture with eBay while taking over eBay China's operations, it felt like a fire sale.

When eBay's announcement hit our in-boxes, the reaction inside Alibaba's offices was subdued. There were no cheers or high fives. Just a calm acceptance and sense of satisfaction at what by that time was a foregone conclusion. As I boarded a plane home for Christmas, I picked up a copy of the *Wall Street Journal* and read the headline, "EBay Steps Back from Asia, Will Shutter China Site." When I changed planes in San Francisco, I picked up the *New York Times* and found its story: "EBay Is Expected to Close Its Auction Site in China."

We had done it, I thought. We had actually beaten eBay. David had beaten Goliath.

Part of me would miss having such a mighty competitor. But with eBay out of the picture and no real competition in sight, the doors were open for something that Jack had postponed for five years.

ALIMANIA

A FLURRY OF FLASHES LIT UP THE CROWDED ROOM, and the clicking and whirring of cameras hit a crescendo. Security cleared a path through the middle of the crowd, giving the 20 photographers, restrained by a rope line, a direct shot of Jack as he jumped on stage. Jack turned to the cameras and triumphantly held two thumbs up amid cheers and applause from the crowd. "Jack! Jack! Over here, Jack!" the photographers called out as the lights illuminated his face and its ear-to-ear smile.

Behind Jack Alibaba's stock price rose on the ticker board of the Hong Kong Stock Exchange. As we watched, we began to realize that Alibaba.com's IPO had just made the company China's largest Internet business and the fifth most valuable Internet company in the world. And this was just one of the companies in Alibaba Group—Alibaba.com. I could only imagine what the entire company might be worth some day if it went public. Through a long glass window we could see onto the trading floor below, where red-vested traders sat behind computer screens furiously trying to keep up with orders for

Alibaba's stock, the volume of which was beginning to destabilize the stock exchange's computer system.

It had taken seven years longer than Jack had originally planned, but we'd finally taken Alibaba.com public. To get there we'd survived the bursting of the Internet bubble. We'd crushed eBay. We'd clashed swords with Google. And we'd managed to buy Yahoo! China along the way. We hadn't been successful at everything. But we'd been successful enough. And despite our run-ins with the American Internet titans, we'd managed to build China's first global Internet company and pull off the second-largest IPO in Internet history.

After a few minutes Jack and the senior executives of Alibaba.com were called to the floor of the stock exchange for the listing ceremony. Stock exchange officials made a few formal remarks, welcoming Alibaba.com to the Hong Kong Stock Exchange.

Surrounded by traders on the stock exchange floor, Jack stepped up to the microphone and said a few words in Chinese:

"Today is an important step for Alibaba and a giant leap for China's Internet industry. We trust Alibaba.com's IPO will help us better serve our investors, customers, employees, and our country. Going public is like stopping at the gas station to refuel. It's an important milestone but not our final destination. We have come a long way to get here, and still have a long way to go."

I looked around the room at my smartly dressed colleagues, the men in suits and ties, the women in sleek dark dresses. It was hard to believe this was the same rag-tag team I had first met when I decided to join the company on that rainy night back in Shanghai. This was the team that, from the beginning, almost no one had taken seriously. This was the team that had been discounted as a cute novelty in an Internet world dominated by US giants. This was the team that Alibaba's first batch of international managers had tried to push aside to make way for "real management."

Yet these 18 founders had prevailed, and in that moment I couldn't help but think how different my colleagues' lives would have been without the Internet. The Internet had given them an outlet—something their parents never had—for their passion and creativity. Not only had my colleagues changed but China had changed. The very movement that Alibaba had created had spawned a new generation of entrepreneurs, millions of whom bought and sold products online, shared ideas, and educated each other. In a country where free speech still had limits—lots of them—they had found self-expression through a singular company.

As the Internet grew, the very fabric of Chinese society was changing. Despite government firewalls, ordinary Chinese were connecting to the outside world more than ever. They might not yet have Western-style political freedoms, but they had something they never would have had during the Cultural Revolution—self-determination.

After a few minutes Jack returned to the observation room, and our colleagues continued to mill about, congratulating each other and reveling in the moment. Then a colleague tapped me on the shoulder and whispered, "Porter, you'd better get Jack out of here. They're about to open up the restraining line and allow the photographers and journalists to move in. If you don't leave now, Jack's gonna get mobbed."

I eventually coaxed Jack away from the crowd and into the hallway. As we worked our way toward the exit, journalists swarmed us in the hope of getting a few last comments from Jack as he left the stock exchange. I walked at Jack's side, flanking him so we could move past the journalists who buzzed with questions, most of which he didn't have time to answer.

"Jack, are you happy with the stock price?"

"Jack, which of your companies do you plan to take public next?"

"Jack, can I get your autograph?"

As we reached the exit and stepped outside into the bright sunshine, the door shut behind us with a loud *whomp,* sealing out the chatter behind us and propelling us into a sudden and eerie silence. It was an exciting day that I didn't want to end. But the IPO was now behind us, and there would be no turning back.

With a wry smile Jack turned to me. "So where do we go next?"

Good question, I thought. I had no answer. Given the tumultuous ride of the previous eight years, it was hard to believe we'd gotten even this far.

LEAVING ALIBABA

WORKING IN A FAST-GROWING START-UP IS A BIT like running a marathon. It's an endurance test, filled with highs and lows. At times you want to give up. And at times you feel the wind at your back. It pushes you to your limits—mentally, physically, and emotionally. It always requires 100 percent commitment, and there is no such thing as cruise control.

The only thing more difficult than deciding when to join a start-up is deciding when to leave. It's hard to leave something you've put so much of your heart into. But it's important to recognize when it's time to take a step back and pass the baton.

As we entered 2008, I realized it was time for me to pass the baton. With the IPO of Alibaba.com we'd reached an important milestone. And with eBay no longer in the China market, the field was wide open, and Taobao had a strong head start, way beyond our competition. It seemed a natural time to take a break. During the nearly eight years I'd worked at Alibaba, I'd moved six times for the company. And I was on the road about 50 percent of the time. I'd loved every minute of it but wanted to have more time for friends, family, and relationships outside

Alibaba. It was tough to tell Jack and Joe Tsai I'd be leaving the company. But they were understanding and asked that I stick around while they looked for a successor.

Despite my sadness it was nice to see that I was leaving behind a company that was in good shape. And it was encouraging to see that the company was energized and in a celebratory mood by the time the 2008 all-hands kickoff meeting ushered in the Year of the Rat. The entire Alibaba staff piled into a large arena for a raucous event filled with speeches and performances punctuated by cheering and the chanting of "A-li-ba-ba, A-li-ba-ba."

It was the first time we'd all gathered since the IPO, and the staff surely felt Alibaba was poised for global dominance. As the day of performances and celebrations came to an end, Jack took the round stage in the center of the arena to address the employees who surrounded him. Ever the contrarian, Jack's message was a sobering one, meant to both inspire and humble the staff.

> We need to be looking out ten years. In ten years people won't be talking about "the Internet" or "e-commerce." It will be a part of our daily lives. We have only ten years to make Alibaba great, because in ten years the infrastructure for e-commerce will already be built. After that it will be too late.
>
> So many companies rise and fall quickly. The environment changes so quickly. A few years ago Yahoo! was our hero. Who would have ever imagined that it would fall from its pedestal to be where it is today? So many of our heroes from yesterday have come and gone. In ten years, when people talk about e-commerce, we want them to be talking about

Alibaba. We don't want people to look back and say, "Alibaba was once a great company."

We must stick to our promises. Today you've begun to have a little money. You've begun to have a little prestige. Don't change because other people see you differently. Don't change because you have money in your pocket. Because there is one thing that can never change: our dreams, our values, and our promises.

2007 was a great year for Alibaba, ending with the exclamation mark of our B2B IPO. Alibaba's social impact is huge. But we have to remember that we are still a small company, not a big company. We are small, but I already notice we are sometimes wasteful. We are small but sometimes we move too slowly. We should prepare for any crisis, and if that crisis comes, we all need to ask, "What can we do to help the company?"

We want it to be the case that if you have a business, no matter where you are, you can plug into Alibaba's ecosystem. We need to be bigger than Walmart someday. Some of you think that is crazy. But one thing is for sure: if you don't imagine it, it will never happen.

Maybe you think that our outlook is great, the economy is great, the stock market is great, and Alibaba is doing really well. But I want to tell you that 2008 is going to be a difficult year. Why did we go public last year? Because we sense that a winter is coming and we have to prepare.

In 2008 Alibaba is going to lie low and prepare for a new winter. And during this winter we have to remember our goals from long ago—to be the last man standing. No matter what, we must be the last man standing.

The crowd applauded his somewhat dire prediction. We had learned from experience that high moments usually preceded low moments. But I took comfort in the knowledge that the team still powered ahead and that Jack had not lost his fire. He'd come a long way from that first time I'd seen him give a speech on a rainy Shanghai night. Just as Alibaba had changed, Jack had changed—from a starry-eyed English teacher into a poised and confident CEO.

Six months later I was in my Beijing office packing personal items in boxes and cleaning out my desk. The team in Hong Kong had offered to organize a going away party for me, but I had declined—it was just too hard to say good-bye to something that had meant so much to me. I thought my departure might go unmarked, but on the morning of my last day Jack's assistant called to let me know that Jack was in Beijing and wanted to take me to lunch.

Over wonton noodles at the China World Hotel, Jack and I shared a few laughs and reflected on the time we'd worked together.

"So what do you plan to do next?" he asked.

"Take some time off to travel, and then I want to spend some time sharing my experiences at Alibaba with entrepreneurs and students. So I hope it's still okay with you that I write a book or make a documentary about my experience here."

"Sure," he said. "You're probably the best person to do it. You've seen the international side and the China side of things."

"But you realize, Jack, don't you, that even though I had a positive experience, I'm going to tell the good and the bad, the successes and the mistakes, from my own perspective?"

"I know," he said with a smile. "Alibaba has a responsibility to share our experience with others, so they can learn from us."

Most CEOs would have been paranoid about the idea that a former employee would be sharing the company's inside story. But at his core Jack was still a teacher.

We shook hands and I headed home. It meant a lot that he'd made the effort to give me a proper thanks and good-bye. I'd joined Alibaba thinking I might learn something about business. But the most valuable things I'd learned from Jack were about life.

WINTER

AFTER LEAVING ALIBABA, I TOOK TIME TO TRAVEL.
After living in China for so long, I used it as a way to remind
myself that there was a whole world out there beyond China's
Great Wall. But Jack's predictions of a winter for the company
soon proved all too prescient. And as I read the headlines, I
couldn't help but feel some regret, that maybe I'd quit the fight
before the job was done.

At about the time I was packing up my office, Lehman
Brothers collapsed. Only later would it become clear just how
much the global economy would suffer. During the next couple
of years, as the global economy melted down, exports from China cooled off, directly impacting Alibaba.com's customer base.
With exporters struggling to stay afloat, they cut their advertising on Alibaba.com, which put downward pressure on Alibaba.
com's stock. Within a year Alibaba's once high-flying stock had
lost nearly 90 percent of its value, falling from HK$40 per share
to almost HK$4 per share.

But even that paled in comparison to the next blow—a scandal among Alibaba's sales team involving criminal fraud. To

Jack's dismay he and Alibaba's senior managers discovered that 100 sales team members had knowingly signed up shady suppliers and certified 2,300 storefronts as Gold Suppliers, even though they didn't meet Alibaba's qualifications. Some of the illegitimate suppliers had gone on to defraud international buyers using Alibaba.com. Savio Kwan, who had years earlier left the COO position and recently returned to Alibaba as a member of Alibaba.com's board of directors, was brought in to lead the company's internal investigation and described the situation in dire terms: "The company was at risk of developing a culture of pursuing short-term financial gain at all cost."[1]

Jack's reaction to the scandal was swift. Once he knew the full scope of the problem, he called for Alibaba.com's CEO, David Wei, and COO, Elvis Lee, to resign. Although they weren't personally implicated in the crime, Jack felt he had to send a strong signal to the market because the company had built its reputation on trust and because he believed that the top executives had to take responsibility for allowing an environment in which this could occur.

A series of other crises followed. When Taobao adjusted the policies on its Tmall shopping website to favor larger, more qualified sellers over smaller, less professional ones, hundreds of Taobao users assembled outside its offices and held demonstrations against the company. Public demonstrations of any kind were highly unusual in China, and the government stepped in to assert itself in the dispute, reprimanding Jack for changing Taobao's policies too quickly.

But no controversy was quite as big as the spin-off of Alibaba's AliPay unit as a separate entity owned and controlled by Jack Ma and Simon Xie, an Alibaba cofounder. When I first read a headline saying that AliPay had been spun off, I was relieved. Throughout my time at Alibaba I had always conservatively valued AliPay at zero. Although it was the circulatory system of Alibaba Group's ecosystem, it was the one business unit that was operating in a regulatory gray area without an official license from banking regulators. The risk was that China's banks would lobby their government allies to have AliPay shut down. And if this happened, the result would have been disastrous, in effect shutting down the majority of transactions on Taobao and imperiling millions of jobs that depended on Alibaba's ecosystem. So when I read that AliPay had been spun off, I assumed that Jack and Alibaba had at last found a way to navigate the banking regulations and that spinning it off was simply a prelude to AliPay's obtaining a license.

But the way in which the transfer was handled led to an acrimonious and highly public battle between Yahoo! and Alibaba about whether or not Jack had secured proper board approval before transferring AliPay into a separate company. Although I understood Jack and viewed his motivation as simply to comply with local regulations by transferring AliPay to a local entity, to outside observers the transfer fit all too neatly the stereotype of Chinese business people who would try to cheat their foreign partners. After months of negotiating, Alibaba and its investors ultimately solved the problem, but the controversy left a black mark on Alibaba's record and damaged a lot of the goodwill that Alibaba had generated over the years.

By the time I sat down with Jack again, three years after I left Alibaba, it was clear that the controversies had taken their toll. In the fall of 2011 I met with Jack in Berkeley, where he was taking time off from China and in many ways Alibaba as well. The good news was that Taobao and its sister site Tmall were continuing to grow exponentially; Taobao alone had surpassed eBay's global transaction volumes. But running such a large company that so many people's livelihoods depended upon forced Jack to confront the reality that he was never going to please everyone. Jack looked worn out and spoke without his usual spark. "When you have 400 million people using the Internet in China," he lamented. "If we set a policy that 99 percent of the people like but only 1 percent of the people don't like, that still means there are four million people angry at us."

The only time I'd ever seen Jack so down was when we had traveled to the US to lay off the Silicon Valley staff. But he'd foreseen this winter of discontent. And he'd always told us, "Today is tough. Tomorrow is tougher. The day after tomorrow is beautiful. But most people die tomorrow night and don't get the chance to see the sun rise the day after tomorrow."

As dark as the winter was, the global currents that had set Alibaba on its path all those years ago were still in force. I knew it was only a matter of time before spring returned to Alibaba.

SPRING

I SETTLED INTO MY HOTEL ROOM FOR THE NIGHT, unpacked my bags, and flipped on the TV. 2013 had gotten off to a good start and I'd had a busy week of traveling around to universities to screen the documentary film I'd made, *Crocodile in the Yangtze: The Alibaba Story.* For the 12 months I'd been showing the film audiences seemed to like it but there was one person whose opinion of the film I was not quite sure of—Jack Ma. After I'd completed the film and was preparing to screen it at festivals and universities, I had shown it to Jack as a courtesy. His original response was lukewarm, so as I sat in my hotel and saw my cell phone ringing with an unexpected call from Jack, I was nervous.

"Porter, where are you these days?" Jack asked.

"In Pittsburgh. What's up?"

"Can you be in Hangzhou on May 10?"

"Maybe," I hedged, waiting to see what he had in mind. "What's going on?"

"We're having a big celebration for Taobao's ten-year anniversary. I'd really like you to come back to attend the party and show your film to the team in Hangzhou."

I was relieved. I'd made my film to inspire entrepreneurs, not to please Jack. But I was always a bit worried about whether Jack thought it was a fair portrait. It was nice to know I hadn't burned any bridges and that, despite his initial reservations about the film, it had grown on him over time. So I was honored that he'd invited me back to the company for Taobao's birthday celebration.

A couple months later I was walking through the tall stadium arches and onto the field of Hangzhou's Yellow Dragon stadium to see what had become of the company I'd left five years earlier. The stadium was packed with a crowd of more than 20,000 employees, customers, and their friends and families. The crowd waved flashing neon glow sticks that were like stars sparkling in the night as fireworks shot into the sky. Acrobats suspended in midair flew across the stadium, their martial arts gowns flowing behind them. And then, rising from a trap door in the stage, emerged the star of the night—Jack—dressed in a Bruno Mars costume and singing "China I Love You" to a wild roar of applause.

It was immediately clear that Alibaba's winter was over. Springtime had arrived. Jack and Alibaba were back.

In the two years since I'd seen the subdued Jack in Berkeley, the company had healed the many wounds it had suffered. Jack's swiftness in replacing Alibaba.com's CEO after the company's sales scandal had helped Alibaba regain the confidence of its customers. As Alibaba.com's share price recovered, Jack chose to take Alibaba.com private, delisting it from the Hong Kong Stock Exchange and absorbing it back into the Alibaba Group, allowing the website to refocus on customers and exploit synergies with other Alibaba companies. After Marissa Mayer became CEO of Yahoo! in July 2012, her arrival renewed the spirit of partnership between the two companies, allowing them to move beyond the AliPay issue. And the Taobao/Tmall controversy ultimately blew over as well, allowing Alibaba's consumer arm to continue its meteoric growth.

As Taobao employees and customers gathered that night to celebrate its ten-year anniversary, they had good reason to cheer. From its modest beginnings Taobao's transaction volumes had grown to become larger than eBay's and Amazon's combined. Looking back on my first visit to Taobao, on that hot day with no air-conditioning when the company was nothing more than a few founders trying to make do without electricity, I found it hard to believe just how far Taobao had come. Its impact was stretching beyond China's cities and towns, transforming entire villages that had begun to adopt e-commerce. Along the way Taobao was fulfilling the team's goal of creating millions of jobs across China for the entrepreneurs who were setting up shops online. Like a small country, its community of members had taken on a life of its own, giving rise to its own celebrities, opinion leaders, even panels of Taobao members elected from within the user base to arbitrate trade disputes between members.

Taobao's birthday party was more than just a celebration for Taobao—it was an important milestone for Jack. He had chosen the event to announce his official resignation as CEO of Alibaba Group. At the end of the night he handed control of the company to Jonathan Lu, a former Holiday Inn front desk clerk who had risen up Alibaba's ranks from a sales position. Jack was stepping down from his CEO position while retaining the role of company chairman. Giving up his title of CEO would allow Jack to manage the company's vision and big-picture issues without having to get bogged down with the day-to-day operational details. And, just as important, the move cleared the way for Alibaba to pursue an IPO of the entire Alibaba Group.

For the next several months I followed Alibaba's developments in the headlines. The company's original goal of having its IPO in Hong Kong proved not to be possible when the regulators of the Hong Kong Stock Exchange refused to approve Alibaba's unique but controversial corporate structure, whereby control of the company would ultimately remain in the hands of Jack Ma and 26 other members of the "Alibaba Partnership" rather than in the hands of ordinary shareholders. Approving such a structure would mean approving an exception to the Hong Kong Stock Exchange policy that allocates shareholder control according to "one share, one vote."

Of the many great reasons for Alibaba to list on the Hong Kong exchange, the most critical was that being listed on Chinese soil would help Alibaba with its relationship with the government as Alibaba moved into highly regulated industries such as finance and media. Listing in Hong Kong had the additional advantage of helping Alibaba managers deal with investors and analysts who were more likely to be based in Alibaba's time zone and thus more familiar with China's business and regulatory environment. But after Alibaba engaged in a heated public debate with the Hong Kong Stock Exchange, its regulators decided not to make an exception for Alibaba's structure. Alibaba ultimately chose the New York Stock Exchange for its listing.

For the next 12 months the slow drumbeat heralding Alibaba's IPO picked up its tempo as the world began to recognize the scale of Alibaba's business and the impact it was having in

China. IPO day, September 19, 2014, arrived at last. I was in Arizona, 2,000 miles from New York, and set my alarm for five a.m. When I woke up, I turned on the TV to watch the entire day of coverage. It was the biggest IPO in history, and when trading started, the company was valued at more than $220 billion. No longer was it just the transaction volumes, but now the company's entire value exceeded eBay and Amazon combined making Alibaba almost as valuable as Walmart. Watching Jack and my former colleagues triumph on the floor of the New York Stock Exchange was like watching former teammates win the Super Bowl.

As the opening bell rang, Jack was ushered into the CNBC broadcast booth, where US viewers got their first real introduction to the world's new king of e-commerce.

Jim Cramer asked, "What does this mean for the People's Republic of China?"

"I think we are giving a lot of people inspiration," Jack responded. "Fifteen years ago I told my people in my apartment that if Jack Ma and people like us can be successful, 80 percent of the people in China can be successful. And 80 percent of young people in the world can be successful. We do not have a rich daddy or powerful uncle. We started from nothing. . . . A lot of young people don't have dreams anymore. And we want to tell them, you have to keep your dreams."

"Jack, this is a great American story that is also a Chinese story. Who are your heroes?"

"The hero I have is Forrest Gump."

The CNBC team laughed, taken aback by Jack's surprising choice. "Box of chocolates?" Cramer asked.

"Yeah, I really like that guy. I've watched that movie about ten times. It taught me that no matter whatever changed, *you* are *you*. And I'm still the guy I was 15 years ago when I only earned $20 per month."

Well said, Jack, I thought as I watched. *Just be yourself. It's what got you this far.*

ALIBABA'S WORLD

DESPITE ITS TRANSFORMATIVE IMPACT IN CHINA,
Alibaba's first 15 years largely went unnoticed in the West. That
all changed with Alibaba Group's massive IPO. As the West
scrambled to understand Alibaba, commentators and analysts
reached for an apt comparison. Was Alibaba's business model
the "Amazon of China," "eBay of China," "PayPal of China,"
"Google of China," or "all of the above"?

These comparisons might be helpful references, but ultimately
they all fall short. That's because, while Alibaba's business model
does incorporate some characteristics of its Western counterparts, it's unique—and innovative in the truest sense of the word.

So what is Alibaba? How should we understand it? How
might it grow? And what will be its future influence on global
e-commerce? To understand this it is helpful to look closely at
Alibaba's core businesses.

ALIBABA GROUP TODAY

The Alibaba Group today is a vast e-commerce conglomerate that connects buyers with sellers and enables them to do

transactions across a wide range of products and services. It operates wholesale and retail marketplaces, which, together with Alibaba's support services (which range from online payment to logistics), increasingly provides the infrastructure for China's modern economy. More than just a collection of related e-commerce businesses, Alibaba has become an ecosystem in which the whole is far greater than the sum of its parts because of the synergies among its elements. Alibaba's ecosystem is comprised of three main elements:

- Wholesale marketplaces
- Retail marketplaces
- Support services provided by ecosystem participants

Wholesale Marketplaces

Alibaba China (1688.com)

Alibaba China (also known as 1688.com) is in many ways the hidden gem of Alibaba Group. I say *hidden* because it is so little known and understood outside China. Although it is one of the two original marketplaces Alibaba started in 1999, Alibaba China has gone largely unnoticed by Westerners, who rarely venture beyond Alibaba's English website, Alibaba.com. Yet in China 1688.com is a massive phenomenon and integral to the Chinese economy.

Alibaba China is China's largest wholesale marketplace for domestic trade, a community of millions of small- and medium-sized manufacturers and trading companies that buy and sell in wholesale volumes. Members use the site to post products, negotiate through live chat and messaging, and, increasingly, consummate their transactions through AliPay. If you must have a Western comparison, think "eBay of wholesale" for the China market. It's largely a subscription-based service; members pay an annual fee to become a premium member with access to Alibaba China's full range of services. It also makes money from pay-for-performance advertising whereby sellers can bid for ads to appear when certain keywords are searched on the site.

The business model is unique, with no clear parallel anywhere in the world (although in certain developing countries with large manufacturing bases and a fragmented wholesale network, there certainly should be).

By the time of Alibaba's 2014 IPO, Alibaba China had more than 700,000 paying members and generated US$22.7 billion in transactions that were settled through AliPay—and that's only a fraction of the total number of deals that originate on Alibaba China. But the numbers alone don't tell the full story. Alibaba China is in many ways more than just a platform—it is a rich and vibrant community whose members regularly post advice on message boards and meet offline to deepen friendships and discuss business. China's transformation to a market economy happened so quickly that Alibaba China stepped up to bring together business people in specialized industries—a role filled in the West by trade associations that have developed over decades.

Alibaba China's importance in the larger Alibaba universe cannot be overstated. Wholesalers on Alibaba China provide much of the product sold by retailers on Taobao and by global exporters on Alibaba.com. Alibaba China's deep links with Alibaba's other marketplaces create incentives for participants to stay within the Alibaba ecosystem. Alibaba China also provides an attractive customer base for Alibaba's financial services, as Alibaba ventures into microcredit, banking, and wealth management.

Alibaba International

Alibaba International (otherwise known as Alibaba.com) is the world's largest wholesale marketplace for global trade, connecting importers and exporters in more than 240 countries and territories. This site is the first thing Westerners see when they click to Alibaba.com, and in many ways it is the flagship site of Alibaba Group. Because its core customers are wholesalers, rather than end consumers, Alibaba.com is not a household name outside China. But nearly everyone in the world has likely used a product sourced on Alibaba.com, which supplies the world's wholesalers with products ranging from ball bearings to coffee mugs to iPhone cases.

From day one Alibaba set out to connect buyers and sellers from around the world, making it the first global Internet company to emerge from China. It's often misunderstood as being a website that only connects Chinese manufacturers to international buyers. In truth, while Chinese exporters form the core of the revenue base, the marketplace's sellers come from all around the world. So, for example, a buyer in France might order shoes from a manufacturer in India. A buyer in Kenya might purchase rugs from a seller in Pakistan. As of the date of the Alibaba Group IPO, Alibaba.com counted more than 120,000 paying members, with millions more who use the website's free services.

Consumer Marketplaces

Taobao.com

Taobao (treasure hunt) is China's largest consumer-to-consumer marketplace. At the time of Alibaba Group's IPO, Alexa.com listed it as one of the ten most-visited websites in the world. Every day more than 100 million people visit Taobao to buy and sell just about every product or service imaginable, accounting for an estimated 80 percent of the online retail sales in China (along with its sister site, Tmall). Taobao has become a part of everyday life for the Chinese, who use it for everything from fashion to movie tickets to groceries from their local convenience store. And as Chinese consumers have increasingly adopted smartphones, Taobao's mobile app has seen a huge volume of sales and purchases.

Although often compared to eBay, Taobao plays a much larger role in China's economy than its American counterpart does in the US economy. Most items sold on Taobao are new items sold on a fixed-price basis, as opposed to eBay, which is largely known as an auction site for secondhand goods and collectibles. The difference owes to the early days of Taobao, when China's retail environment consisted of millions of small- and medium-sized businesses and mom-and-pop shops, as well as large retail chains and department stores. Taobao effectively gave these small retailers a place to market their wares online while also improving upon the offline shopping experience by introducing features such as instant messaging and elaborate seller rating systems that allowed for convenience, communication, and trust building.

Taobao's website reflects the local culture and shopping habits of Chinese consumers. Compared to the home pages of Western websites, Taobao's looks busy, with flashing icons and animated cartoon characters promoting special deals. If clicking through eBay is like a walk down Main Street, USA, clicking through Taobao is like a walk down Shanghai's busy Nanjing Lu, where sights and sounds bombard the shopper. To Western eyes Taobao's home page might seem too cute or flashy, even distracting, but it is what Chinese users prefer and expect.

Taobao's marketplace offers another important feature that sets it apart from many of its Western counterparts—shoppers are able to immediately click through to the seller and initiate a live chat. This is not surprising—the Chinese are accustomed to building a relationship with a seller before making a purchase, and in China's shopping culture haggling and negotiation are standard. Whereas prices in an eBay auction start low and get bid up, prices on Taobao often start high and get haggled down. In fact, it's hard to imagine e-commerce thriving in China without Taobao's popular Wang Wang live chat feature.

The most important of Taobao's features are those that allow online buyers and sellers to establish trust. Like eBay, Taobao allows buyers to rate the services of sellers after a transaction. Taobao's ratings system tends to be much more extensive, allowing buyers to rate their sellers on many more variables. This reflects China's lack of credit infrastructure and has led to Taobao's filling the void often filled in North America by private companies and nonprofit organizations such as the Better Business Bureau. In conjunction with AliPay, Taobao has become the best source of rating and credit information for small businesses in China.

Taobao's monetization model sets it apart from its Western counterparts'. Instead of taking a commission from each transaction, Taobao makes money by offering sellers ways to promote themselves, such as through premium storefronts, keyword advertisements, and other advertising opportunities. Because of its history as a largely free service, Taobao has introduced fees slowly over time, opting for a more conservative "take rate" on Taobao which captures less than 2.5 percent of a transaction's value versus eBay's take rate of 8.5 percent. But Taobao's contribution to the Alibaba ecosystem is a powerful one, because it maintains a strong relationship with customers that can mean more money in Alibaba's pocket through its other services, such as Tmall or AliPay.

Tmall

In many ways small, scrappy entrepreneurs built e-commerce in China through their storefronts on Taobao. Students or small retailers had more incentive than a behemoth to take to the Internet, because it brought them to the attention of potential buyers from all over China. Although small retailers were quick to embrace and pioneer e-commerce, large brands and retailers were slow, because e-commerce initially represented such a small percentage of their overall sales.

However, once Taobao was established as China's largest shopping destination, large brands and retailers began to pay attention. At the same time many consumers were receiving uneven levels of service from the small retailers on Taobao and wanted a way to go directly to a large retailer or brand owner. "Why buy a product from a small corner shop and risk the product's being a refurbished or damaged one when you can buy directly from a large, reputable retailer?" they thought.

With this situation in mind Alibaba Group introduced Tmall. com, a marketplace that connects large brands and retailers directly with consumers. The site opened in April 2008 as a part of Taobao and became an independent platform in 2011. As of June 30, 2014, it featured 110,000 brands and described itself as "dedicated to providing a premium shopping experience for Chinese consumers in search of top-quality branded merchandise." If Taobao is a flea market with scrappy entrepreneurs hawking their wares, Tmall is the shiny shopping mall with glossy storefronts and dedicated sales and customer service staff.

One of the main benefits of Tmall for Alibaba Group is monetization. Whereas the fiercely independent and cost-conscious sellers on Taobao are highly resistant to paying commissions, fees, or anything that might seem like a tax on their sales, the large brands and retailers on Tmall typically are more than happy to pay commissions of around 5 percent to Alibaba Group for each sale. To them a few percentage points is a small price to pay to reach hundreds of millions of consumers in an online environment that bypasses the expensive retail and logistics infrastructure to which they are accustomed in the offline world.

Tmall has become an important channel for foreign brands to establish a presence in China and reach customers in China's interior, where their retail infrastructure has yet to be built out. Brands such as Gap, Levis, Adidas, and Ray Ban have stores in Tmall and often use their Tmall shops as a way to learn about local customers while exploring how to further grow their presence in the market.

Tmall gets credit for pioneering China's November 11 Singles' Day promotion, a shopping day when consumers receive discounts. On November 11, 2014, Tmall and Taobao generated $9.3 billion in sales. Alibaba Group has made "going global" a major theme for Tmall and is increasingly recruiting foreign brands to sell on the marketplace.

Juhuasuan

Before there was Groupon, there was Taobao's Group Buy feature, which allowed groups of friends to negotiate for a volume discount from sellers. Group Buy reflected the social nature of commerce in China, combining China's group-oriented culture with the Chinese habit of haggling to get better prices on goods.

The trend of leveraging the power of group purchases to reduce product prices became so strong on Taobao that in 2010 the company started Juhuasuan as a separate group-buying marketplace that offers products at discounted prices by aggregating demand from numerous consumers, often through flash sales. Despite competition from hundreds of similar sites that popped up as Groupon gained attention in the West, Juhuasuan emerged as China's most popular online group-buying marketplace, largely as a result of the relationships that Alibaba Group had with its existing customers on Taobao and AliPay.

AliExpress

AliExpress is Alibaba's first attempt to connect Chinese sellers directly with consumers in international markets. Begun in April 2010, it showcases a wide variety of products at wholesale prices from wholesalers and manufacturers in China. By June 30, 2014, it was generating annual sales of US$4.5 billion, catering largely to consumers in emerging markets such as Russia, Brazil, and Nigeria.

Support Services Provided by Ecosystem Participants

Ant Financial Services Group

In October 2014, Alibaba Group launched Ant Financial Services Group, putting AliPay and its many related financial and credit services under a new roof. The name "Ant" is meant to refer to the small and micro-sized businesses the company serves, filling a void neglected by China's state-backed banks, which tend to serve China's state-owned enterprises. Among Ant Financial Services, AliPay is the shining star, having grown to become the world's largest third-party online payment provider, quickly approaching $1 trillion in annual transaction volumes. It offers both direct and escrow-based payments for buyers and sellers engaged in domestic China transactions as well as cross-border transactions. AliPay facilitates transactions with Alibaba Group marketplaces as well as transactions for third-party merchants and service providers. Users can set up payments for utilities, mobile phone charges, rent, tuition, fees, and peer-to-peer fund transfers.

AliPay's mobile service, AliPay Wallet, is increasingly replacing cash in China, supporting offline payments by allowing users to electronically transfer funds through advanced technologies including QR codes and sound wave payment. People are using AliPay Wallet at offline shops, restaurants, vending machines, taxis, and cinema chains. It is quickly becoming a routine part of life with such features as allowing a group of friends to split a bill equally at a restaurant through its Go Dutch feature.

China's inefficient state-run banking system allowed Ant Financial (and its predecessor, Small and Micro Financial Services) to move into related areas more aggressively than have other payment systems, such as PayPal in the West. For example, when the company opened a money market fund, Yu'e Bao (leftover treasure), in June 2013, it quickly attracted 125 million users with interest rates that exceeded those at China's traditional banks. Those users invested RMB570 billion in the fund. So while AliPay was launched as a payment system, it has evolved into a much larger and more diversified provider of financial services.

Alibaba Group describes Ant Financial as a "related company" because of its arm's-length ownership structure, which was designed to comply with China's heavily regulated financial industry. Through this complicated structure, Alibaba Group receives favorable terms for AliPay services while retaining an ownership stake and long-term claim to a portion of AliPay (and Ant Financial) profits.

Logistics

Logistics inefficiencies in China present both challenges and opportunities for e-commerce companies. While Western markets like the US are served by established national delivery services such as DHL, UPS, and FedEx, China's logistics landscape is much more fragmented, with the market divided between several different players with varying levels of reliability and coverage. So it's no surprise that China's logistics providers have scrambled to catch up to the e-commerce boom, which saw more than 250 million packages shipped in the days after the 2014 Singles' Day promotion.

To address the logistical challenges of keeping up with the demands of China's fast-growing e-commerce market, Alibaba brought together the five major express delivery companies in China to set up a separate entity, China Smart Logistics Network, of which Alibaba owns 48 percent. The goal is to align and coordinate the logistics players to more seamlessly fulfill orders.

Alibaba's approach differs from that of China's leading on-line retailer, Jingdong.com, which has been building its own warehousing and distribution network, allowing it to control the customer experience from end to end. This has set up competition between Alibaba's loosely allied network and the vertically integrated Jingdong. But perhaps the bigger race will be between the physical delivery infrastructure and the digital infrastructure, which is growing so quickly that it is straining China's logistics system and risks creating a short-term bottleneck for the growth of e-commerce.

Media and Entertainment

As the son of a Pingtan performer, Jack Ma has a flair for the dramatic. So it's not surprising that Alibaba is making an aggressive move into media and entertainment, investing in the video-sharing site Youku Tudou and establishing a film production company, Alibaba Pictures. To outside observers this may seem like a step away from Alibaba's core strength. But in the context of China, the deal may make sense.

The way to think of Alibaba's move into film and entertainment is this: If it is a product that can be bought and sold online, you can expect Alibaba will want to be there. And film and video are products that can be bought and sold online. E-commerce marketplaces traditionally have sold physical products. But increasingly they are becoming marketplaces for digital products, such as books, films, tickets, and virtual products used in video games. So it's not surprising that Alibaba Group is interested in selling video products online through its digital platforms.

Alibaba's more ambitious move is into the area of content production. To explain his move into film production, Jack told the *South China Morning Post* that in China "people's wallets are bulging but their heads are empty."[1] It's not an area entirely new to Jack, as he sits on the board of directors of Huayi Brothers Media Corporation, producers of the China blockbusters *Cell Phone* and *A World without Thieves*. Now that China has the world's second-largest box office, behind the US, film has become a lucrative business providing real returns. Beyond that, Jack has a personal interest in bringing film into the lives of the Chinese. "E-commerce can affect people's wallets. But film can affect people's minds," he once told me.

Other Support Services

Beyond these core products and services, Alibaba owns and/or is invested in a wide variety of businesses. Its homegrown cloud computing arm, AliCloud, provides computing power and storage for app developers and merchants, while its AliMama division provides Big Data analytics for marketers. Alibaba Group also has been acquiring and investing in companies in a range of areas, from mobile web browsers to retail to microblogging. Through these aggressive investments and acquisitions Alibaba is hoping to expand its reach so that each of these related companies further enhances the links between, and network effects of, the ecosystem. But in some corners the company's aggressive expansion has met resistance from analysts who argue it may be going too far, notably with its nearly $200 million investment in a Guangzhou football team, Evergrande.

Alibaba Group Tomorrow

By the time of its IPO Alibaba was 15 years old. For many companies this would be considered reaching the age of maturity. But compared with the company's stated goal Alibaba is a mere teenager. Thinking that his original goal for Alibaba to last 80 years was too conservative, Jack later extended the goal to 102 years, noting that it would allow Alibaba's life to span three centuries. If this ambitious goal is to be reached, then Alibaba still has more than 85 years left to go. If Alibaba does manage to live this long, how might it grow? And what might Alibaba become someday?

Alibaba's stated vision is nothing less than to build "the future infrastructure of commerce," serving its mission to "make it easy to do business anywhere." It wants to build a place where people will meet, work, and even "live" online so that the company's products and services become central to the everyday lives of its customers. Given these goals and Alibaba's past history, here are some of the main trends we might expect to see Alibaba focusing on in the future.

Growth of Alibaba's Core Businesses

When Alibaba Group went public, only about half of China's population of 1.36 billion was online. And of those Internet users, only about half had shopped online. It's amazing to think that with only about 25 percent of China's population, or 302 million, shopping online, Alibaba's consumer sales volumes already exceed those of Amazon and eBay combined. One can only imagine the scale if these growth trends continue as more of China's population comes online and takes to Internet shopping. It's reasonable to argue that China's e-commerce industry is in many ways still in its infancy and we can expect that Alibaba will continue to focus on China as it grows its main businesses, Alibaba.com, Alibaba China, Taobao, Tmall, and AliPay.

While growing these core businesses, it will be important for the company to stay ahead of one major wave that is reshaping e-commerce in China—the shift from PCs to mobile shopping. Although its start on mobile was slower than its competitors', Alibaba has managed to grow and build a leadership position in mobile commerce. Holding that position and monetizing mobile will be crucial.

Growth of Alibaba's Ecosystem

We can expect Alibaba to continue to grow its ecosystem and plug in more related services, such as cloud computing, logistics, navigation, and mapping. Growing its ecosystem without diluting its core businesses will require the company to find a fine balance. If successful, Alibaba will create a universe held together by the common links between all its services. But in doing so, it needs to avoid overexpansion, which might weaken its main services while creating opportunities for more specialized competitors to chip away at Alibaba's market share.

Expansion into New Industry Frontiers

Perhaps the least-appreciated areas of potential growth for Alibaba are in massive industries that are being deregulated in China. Two major opportunities come to mind: financial services and media.

Anyone who has lived in China can attest to the inefficiency of its banks. One need look no further than the typical bank lobby, where customers wait for as long as an hour in rows of chairs just to pay the rent. By definition any business that creates a waiting room full of chairs is not serving its customers well.

Alibaba's rapid success with its Yu'e Bao money market fund showed the potential for e-commerce players in banking. It's easy to imagine that Internet companies like Alibaba and its rival Tencent could quickly convert their e-commerce customers into clients for financial services, everything from banking, loans, and insurance to wealth management. The big question is how quickly China will deregulate its banks. A hopeful sign for Alibaba came in the fall of 2014, when it received approval from the China Banking Regulatory Commission to establish a privately owned bank.

Another industry ripe for Alibaba's participation is media and entertainment. Like banking, China's media have been dominated by the government since the Communist takeover in 1949. The result is bland state-created media content, which may satisfy government leaders but is not good at meeting the demands of audiences.

The Internet has created a much more open playing field for film and video content in China. While censorship still inhibits growth in certain areas of political content, China's media have become much more market oriented as the Internet has grown. China's youth are much more likely to spend their time watching Internet content in front of the computer than watching staid government-sponsored content in front of the TV with their parents. At the same time China's huge box office makes films aimed at the domestic audience commercially viable.

As government control of media content continues to loosen, we can expect that Internet companies will take up the slack, providing content that is much more market driven. And as distribution moves from cable television to the computer, tablet, and streaming, e-commerce companies such as Alibaba are well positioned to monetize digital products in the same way they monetized physical products. Indeed, immediately after Alibaba's IPO Jack Ma spent time in Hollywood meeting with executives and positioning Alibaba as a gateway to the China market. While it begins to distribute content made by others, Alibaba Pictures will be moving toward producing original content.

Geographic Expansion

Outsiders often overlook or forget that Alibaba has always been a global business, from the day it began in 1999. Because Alibaba's domestic China retail business has so dominated recent headlines about the company, people often forget that, of all of China's Internet companies, Alibaba has the greatest international presence. Alibaba Group already has nearly ten million users in the US, three million in India, two million in Brazil, and half a million in Germany. Thus the question is not whether Alibaba will go global but how Alibaba will continue to go global, especially in its consumer businesses.

As Alibaba headed toward its IPO in New York, a number of journalists asked me whether Alibaba would be "invading" the US and taking on eBay or Amazon directly. My opinion is that Alibaba has learned from the mistakes of its competitors. Just as eBay's US models didn't fit the China market, Taobao's and Tmall's model don't fit the US market. It would be hard to imagine that Alibaba could parachute into the West and compete directly with its Western counterparts. More likely is that Alibaba will first focus on cross-border trade, helping Chinese companies sell abroad through AliExpress and foreign companies sell in China through Tmall. And it's likely that Alibaba will use its growing war chest to make strategic investments in similar e-commerce businesses in other countries.

While I don't expect Alibaba to pose a threat to Western e-commerce giants on their home turf in the near term, one tantalizing possibility should not be ruled out—that Alibaba might acquire one or more of the US giants, such as eBay. These businesses would be entirely complementary, with little overlap. Back in 2003, when reporters asked Jack if he would sell his company to eBay, he would often joke in response: "No, but we might consider buying them." With eBay valued at over $30 billion at the time, and Taobao yet to earn any revenues, it seemed a preposterous claim. But not anymore.

CHALLENGES

Retaining Customers within Its Ecosystem

Alibaba must continue to innovate and provide relevant and powerful services that encourage its buyers and sellers to stay within its ecosystem. Despite all the great opportunities before Alibaba today, Jack and his management team are well aware that the tech road is littered with failed companies who had their brief moment in the sun before they were overtaken by new technologies and entrepreneurs. Alibaba needs to look only as far as its major partner, Yahoo!, which saw Google and Facebook speed past it in search engine usage and social networking, opportunities that Yahoo! had been well positioned to grab for itself, if only the company had had the vision and foresight to do so. In my early days at Alibaba, Jack Ma often quoted Intel's Andy Grove: "Only the paranoid survive." In the tech world at any moment a new idea or gizmo or app can cause a massive industry shift that renders old business models instantly obsolete. Maintaining a healthy level of paranoia will be important for Alibaba's senior management.

An early risk for Taobao was that it might educate the China market about e-commerce only to see retailers break away over time and create their own online retail presence, bypassing Taobao altogether. The introduction of Tmall helped make this less likely by giving sellers the option to create a deeper and much more customized brand experience for their users. Meanwhile services such as AliPay, whose customers have gone to considerable trouble to link their bank accounts to Alibaba's infrastructure, encourage shoppers to stay within the Alibaba ecosystem. Still, some specialized retailers have done well enough to leave the Taobao and Tmall platform and create their own websites, selling directly to customers. Alibaba will have to use all its data, technology, and innovation to offer the best shopping experience in China for a diverse set of products and brands.

Outside Competition

eBay's withdrawal from the China market left several years' worth of running room for Taobao to gain a foothold in the market. But as e-commerce went mainstream, it was only natural that homegrown competition emerged. The most prominent of these competitors is Jingdong.com, whose business-to-customer retail store went live in 2004 and ten years later had about 22 percent of the B2C e-commerce market in China. Unlike Alibaba's marketplace model, whose only inventory is the bits and bytes in its servers, Jingdong is a large retailer modeled after Amazon.com. It has an inventory of products and delivers them through an extensive warehouse and distribution system. Following Amazon's long-term investment strategy, Jingdong spent heavily on expanding its infrastructure, losing money as it grew to scale. By being able to control the customer experience from order to fulfillment, Jingdong is banking on providing a more reliable customer experience than users receive through Taobao or Tmall. It will be interesting to see whether Jingdong's retail model or Alibaba's marketplace model will triumph in the long run. For now investors are betting on Alibaba, but with a market cap of approximately $40 billion at the time of Alibaba Group's IPO, Jingdong is a formidable force in China.

While Jingdong takes on Alibaba directly, others, most notably Tencent, are moving into Alibaba's territory from the side. Like Alibaba, Tencent is a vast conglomerate of Internet businesses, from social networks and messaging to online gaming. Led by its steady and unassuming founder, Pony Ma, Tencent was valued at nearly $150 billion at the time of Alibaba's IPO. Its popular WeChat mobile phone messaging and social networking platform dominates the China market and has allowed Tencent to move aggressively into e-commerce, forcing Alibaba to play catch-up on mobile. Tencent's 15 percent stake in Jingdong brings Alibaba's two biggest competitors together in an alliance that foreshadows the battle ahead.

These three major players constitute about 75 percent of the Chinese B2C e-commerce market, with the remaining 25 percent split between a number of players, none of which has more than 5 percent. Moving forward, the most likely scenario is that more e-commerce players will emerge to take a greater share of the market. But however it shakes out, the heavy investment and intense competition will grow e-commerce in China, to everyone's benefit. And the biggest winners will be consumers, entrepreneurs, and brands. They will have a new and effective channel through which to reach the world's largest market.

Government Regulation

When initiating China's "reform and opening up" policy, Deng Xiaoping famously said, "When you open the door, some flies will come in." The Chinese government opened the door to the Internet because of the economic benefits it can create—e-commerce is a natural fit with the government's goals. But when the door to e-commerce opened, some flies did come in, in the form of political content and the ability of ordinary citizens to mobilize opposition that might challenge the Communist Party's authority.

Outside China, many people seem to think that the government so controls the Internet that they are surprised that e-commerce could take off in China at all, let alone give rise

to the world's largest e-commerce company. But this perception misses a fundamental point: while the government strictly
controls news, information, and communications—areas where
flies are most likely to emerge—it was relatively hands-off in the
more politically neutral area of e-commerce.

Looking back at the effect the Chinese government had on
the development of Alibaba, I can safely say that at times the
government created headwinds and at times it created tailwinds,
but neither were strong enough to be a major factor in Alibaba's
success or failure. More important than any relationship with
the government was the company's relationship with customers.
Building innovative products and services that fit the needs of
entrepreneurs and their customers was what got Alibaba where
it is at today. My strong conviction is that Alibaba succeeded
despite the government, not because of it.

The IPO and Alibaba's size are likely to change the dynam-
ics of its relationship with the government. When it was much
smaller, Alibaba was largely below the radar of the government.
But with so much of the country's GDP flowing through Alibaba's services, the government can't help but pay attention and
probably will approach Alibaba with a giant bear hug in the future, if only to keep it close. Jack's stated goal of "being in love
with the government but not marrying it" will become harder
and harder to maintain over time.

Overall the government is likely to provide Alibaba with a
tailwind as it moves ahead. As homegrown heroes, Jack and
Alibaba are likely to be first in line for licenses in sensitive areas
such as finance and media, despite the heavy presence of foreign
investors in the company's ownership structure. Alibaba's insistence on leaving the company in the hands of its 27 partners

should help allay any government fears that Alibaba could fall into the hands of "outside forces."

But as Alibaba gets closer to the Chinese government, it will have to maintain a delicate balance with Western governments. Since his days as an English teacher, Jack has always considered one of his missions to be the creation of a bridge between China and the outside world. But in an era when China and Western governments are at odds on corporate espionage, government spying, and data privacy, being close to the Chinese government may mean that some of its global expansion efforts will meet a backlash from foreign governments or customers. Alibaba is an easy lightning rod for any and all criticism of China, and, whether he likes it or not, Jack Ma has become the face of China Inc.

THE LEGACY AND GLOBAL IMPACT OF ALIBABA

To understand the impact that Alibaba has had in China, look no further than the one million shops based in rural areas that are active on Taobao and Tmall, selling anything from farm produce to furniture to crafts. Although e-commerce first took root in China's cities among the urban middle class, it has since grown to become a national phenomenon, providing grassroots employment opportunities to drivers, couriers, and web designers deep in China's hinterlands. Some of these mom-and-pop entrepreneurs have since graduated to building national brands.

By 2014 the trend had given rise to 20 "Taobao villages"— defined by Alibaba as villages where more than 10 percent of their households engage in e-commerce and total e-commerce transaction volume in the village exceeds RMB 10 million (about US$1.6 million) per year. The emergence of e-commerce in China's countryside came at an important time, as rural jobs were becoming scarce and the country's most talented and educated youth left the countryside for the cities. In fact e-commerce opportunities in their home villages have lured recent graduates back home to be part of the local e-commerce boom. More than any foreign aid or government initiative, e-commerce has leveled the playing field for entrepreneurs in remote regions, unleashed the entrepreneurial energy of China's rural population, and helped lift entire villages out of poverty.

This trend, along with the emerging middle class, has shown that, although e-commerce was much slower to take off in China, once it finally took root, its impact was much more significant than in the US and Europe. As I noted earlier, while e-commerce proved an *evolutionary* development for commerce in the US, it proved *revolutionary* in China. Just as vast swaths of China leapfrogged directly to cell phones, skipping landlines altogether, China's entire e-commerce ecosystem leapfrogged beyond the West, without first building a traditional and costly physical retail infrastructure.

The good news for other developing countries is that the e-commerce revolution in China's emerging markets is not peculiar to China. Now that China has proven that e-commerce can thrive in developing countries, investors and entrepreneurs in other countries can learn from Alibaba's example. Indeed, while traveling the world during 2014 to screen my documentary film, *Crocodile in the Yangtze: The Alibaba Story*, I noticed an interesting trend. No longer were e-commerce companies in emerging markets calling themselves the Amazon or eBay of their home country. Whether it's the founders of Konga.com in

Nigeria, Flipkart in India, or Tokopedia in Indonesia, the entrepreneurs I've encountered are now more likely to learn from—and compare themselves to—Alibaba.

If the last 20 years was the story of e-commerce in the West, the next 20 years will be the story of e-commerce in the East. Whereas China was once known as an Internet imitator, it is increasingly being rightfully recognized as an e-commerce innovator. China's e-commerce pioneers have become an inspiration for e-commerce entrepreneurs around the world, and China has become an exciting laboratory for new ideas that will have a global impact on e-commerce.

Whether Alibaba succeeds or fails in the long run, Alibaba's greatest contribution to e-commerce may ultimately be that it has developed a new business model that better fits the local conditions of developing markets. By demonstrating that the barriers to e-commerce in the developing world can be overcome, Alibaba has shown that e-commerce entrepreneurs can create a reliable ecosystem for commerce where governments and other institutions have failed. In the past China was best known for its export of cheap goods. But China's most recent export—the Alibaba model—gives hope that the rest of the developing world may be about to enter its own golden era of e-commerce.

ALIBABA AND THE
FORTY LESSONS

WORKING INSIDE ALIBABA TAUGHT ME A LOT ABOUT both business and life. The experiences challenged some of my own assumptions about what people are capable of and taught me that, if they are working in the right conditions, ordinary people with no special backgrounds can go on to create great things. More than anything, it taught me what it takes to achieve a dream and that—yes—some of those corny clichés we learn as children turn out to be true even in the business world. With this in mind I've boiled down what I learned from my experience at the company to the following 40 lessons from the Alibaba story.

ON CHASING A DREAM

Dream Big—Really Big

Whenever Jack asked his managers to set goals for the company, we would provide our most optimistic projections. Jack would usually come back and triple or quadruple our goal. Despite initial resistance from managers, Jack dared them to dream: "If you don't imagine it will happen, it will never happen," Jack told us all. At the end of the year we nearly always found that we had not only met but exceeded those lofty goals.

Never Underestimate Yourself

When I first joined Alibaba, Jack was regularly telling the world that he would resign in four years. "I was trained to be an English teacher, not a CEO," he would say, stressing that he would have to make way for a professional CEO to take over the company. At the same time he told his cofounders that they should not expect to be senior managers in the company, since they had no business experience. Through hard work, self-education, and openness to new ideas, Jack and his cofounders grew and developed into CEOs and senior managers, surprising even themselves. This taught me that in a fast-changing environment such as the Internet, there are no experts and the first place to look for talent is in the mirror and on your existing team.

Never Overestimate Your Competitor

When we started Taobao in Jack's apartment, it would have been easy to be intimidated by our mighty competitor, eBay. It was the market leader and media darling, and it had way more resources. But while large companies like to project an image of strength and dominance, on the inside they typically are much weaker than they look. Just as one should never underestimate oneself, one should never overestimate a competitor.

Make Sure You Have a Great Idea

Jack was an incredibly inspiring leader, but at the core of Alibaba's business was a good idea—connecting buyers and sellers online. All too often entrepreneurs have the passion, the values, and the dream, but they don't have a real core idea for a business. It seems like common sense but no amount of lofty ambition can compensate for an idea that simply doesn't work.

Build a Company to Last 102 Years (at Least)

When I joined Alibaba, Jack was claiming that he wanted us to build a company that would last 80 years—"the length of a human life," he said. Soon thereafter he decided 80 years wasn't long enough and extended the time frame to 102 years, "so that Alibaba would span three centuries." Setting such a long-term goal changes everyone's mind-set. Rather than working quarter to quarter, people strive to achieve the long-term vision.

Remember: The Bigger the Problem, the Greater the Opportunity

E-commerce took off much more quickly in the West than in China, building on an already highly efficient market. In the US and Europe there were far fewer problems to solve. But when Alibaba opened for business in China, the barriers to e-commerce seemed almost insurmountable, and many skeptics said that China simply had too many problems for e-commerce to take off. But after spending years building China's e-commerce infrastructure from the ground up, Alibaba was positioned to capture a greater share of the rewards than its Western counterparts. It had created the market from scratch. As a result, it captured a greater share of the spoils.

Today is Tough but the Day After Tomorrow is Beautiful

One of Jack's favorite sayings proved to be true: "Today is tough, tomorrow is tougher, and the day after tomorrow is beautiful. But most companies die tomorrow evening and can't see the sunshine on the day after tomorrow."

For people to remain oriented to the long term, they must recognize that just as joy is part of a start-up company, so is pain. But the only way to build something great is to endure a lot of struggles.

ON STRATEGY

Focus on the Customer and the Rest Will Follow

Alibaba's credo was always "Customers first, employees second, and investors third." This was a stark contrast to those who argue that a company's primary responsibility is to its shareholders. But the two perspectives are not mutually exclusive. During the B2B Internet bubble, we watched as our competitors followed the expectations of investors and analysts right off a cliff. And in our competition with eBay we recognized that pressure from Wall Street investors would not allow eBay to focus on the long term. It's more important to build products and services that your customers want than to cater to the latest investment fad popular among investors. If you do what is right for your customers and employees, investors will be rewarded in the end.

Learn from Competitors but Never Copy Them

I found it interesting that Jack often refused to read books about competitors. But in some ways, it made sense. Cutting and pasting a business model from one market to another is never innovative. One can learn from competitors, but it's always more important to focus on your customers and build a product and service for them than it is to simply copy your competition. And once you've seen exactly how someone else does it, it's bound to creep into your thinking. As Jack viewed it: "Learn from competitors but never copy them. Copy them and you will die."

Don't Change Rabbits

Another of Jack's favorite sayings is, "If you are a wolf chasing rabbits, focus on one rabbit. Change yourself to catch the rabbit, but don't change rabbits." Companies quickly lose their way when they lose track of their central mission. Despite changing business models and expanding into entirely new areas, Alibaba never lost its focus on its central mission—to make doing business easy.

Be as Fast as a Rabbit but Patient as a Turtle

Entrepreneurs need to work on two different tracks at the same time. On the one hand, they should orient their vision to the long term, like Jack's 102-year company. But on the other hand, they need to move aggressively and quickly day-to-day. The two tracks help keep the company balanced between long-term vision and short-term action.

It's More Important to Be Best than First

Entrepreneurs often come up with an idea but are scared off when they learn that "somebody is already doing that." But being first doesn't always matter as much as people think. Being first to market is not as important as being the best in the market. eBay was first to the market in China, and its managers assumed their first-mover advantage would lead them to victory. But Taobao simply built a better product and prevailed in the long run.

Free Is, Sometimes, a Business Model

When Taobao announced it would be free, eBay was quick to publicly deride the move, arguing that "free is not a business model." But it is sometimes essential to first give your services away for free, especially in the Internet world. This allows businesses to build a critical mass of customers while allowing the management team of the sponsoring company to learn from, and adjust a business model to, the needs of its customers. Think of the great Internet companies of today—almost all started as a free service. Google searches are free. Using Facebook is free. Both companies resisted getting weighed down by gold pieces at the base of the mountain and were rewarded for the decision later, once they reached the peak.

Buy an Umbrella When It's Not Raining

It's the best time, according to Jack. That was why he decided to raise an additional round of financing from Softbank in 2000, before he needed the money. A couple months after he did so, the market crashed and investment for start-ups dried up. Sometimes it's important to prepare for a storm before it comes.

Find Opportunity in Crisis

One of the clichés that litter the expat speaking circuit is that the Chinese word for *crisis* combines the two characters that mean danger and opportunity. But Alibaba's example demonstrates the truth to this concept.

When SARS hit China in 2003, it threatened the company's very survival. When an Alibaba colleague was diagnosed with SARS, 500 employees at company headquarters were sent into quarantine and forced to work remotely from home to operate the company.

But from this danger emerged an opportunity. Alibaba wasn't the only company that had difficulty doing business face to face during that period. Our customers did too. E-commerce was the only way for commerce to continue. We had long worked hard to highlight e-commerce's benefits, but the SARS epidemic greatly accelerated the adoption of e-commerce by China's businesses, and our website traffic reached a new level.

Time and time again we found opportunity in crisis. Rather than being paralyzed by fear of the situation, remaining calm and looking for the opportunity was key.

Use Your Competitor's Strength against It

When eBay announced it was committing $100 million to the China market to compete with us, some within the company, including me, were fearful. Fortunately Jack faced it with a great deal of calm. Channeling his inner martial artist, he realized that a competitor's strength could be used against it. By engaging eBay in a public war of words, we ensured that for each dollar eBay spent in the China market, Chinese consumers and businesses were also learning about Taobao, from the buzz generated by our PR campaign.

Leapfrog

In the past, people observed that China's consumers were leapfrogging from devices such as a landline phone straight to a mobile telephone without having to build out the costly infrastructure of landlines.

Alibaba's experience has shown that entire economic systems can leapfrog ahead, especially in developing countries. Whereas the US and Western Europe spent the last several hundred years developing a retail infrastructure, China's commercial infrastructure was able to leapfrog directly online without retailers first building out an extensive offline retail infrastructure.

In the Spring Prepare for Winter

Alibaba's history is one of bursts of euphoria followed by crisis. Whether it was raising $25 million in financing before the

Internet bubble burst, doing a billion-dollar deal with Yahoo!, or having its IPO in Hong Kong, each new milestone precipitated a crisis.

Alibaba's story arc is not singular—the same thing happened to Google, Facebook, Apple, and Microsoft. David is always a hero until he becomes a Goliath. The time to mentally prepare for the winter is when you are still in the spring.

Resist the Temptation to Go Public

An IPO is a milestone but it should never be the main goal. In 1999, on the day Alibaba was founded, Jack told his team, "The goal is to go public by 2002. If we don't go public by then, then we should forget about it." At the time three years seemed like a long-term goal. But as we got closer to having an IPO, Jack would always resist, telling the staff, "We could go public now, but we should only go public when we are strong enough, otherwise the company will simply fall apart." As Jack put it, "An IPO is like going to the gas station to fill up on gas for a long road ahead."

Put Yourself in Position for Luck

From time to time I encountered people who said that Jack's success was simply due to luck. But more than any of his contemporaries, Jack put himself in the position for luck to find him. Seeing the impact that the Internet could have on China in the long run, Jack decided to dedicate his business career to e-commerce before China was even connected to the Internet. Seeing this trend before others did helped him move his career into position. Despite missing the shot on goal with his first attempt, ChinaPages, he was still standing in front of the goal when the Internet finally took off in China four years later. And when the ball was passed to him the next time, in the form of Alibaba, he kicked it in and scored.

ON LEADERSHIP

Entrepreneurs Don't Complain About Problems—They Solve Them

There are two types of people—those who complain about problems and those who solve them. Sure, we all complain from time to time to vent some steam. But in building a team, it's important to weed out habitual complainers. Habitual complainers fail to realize that they have the power to solve the very problems they are complaining about. At Alibaba, habitual complainers who managed to slip through the interview process didn't last long. Problem solving is the core of entrepreneurship. Problem solving is what entrepreneurial businesses do.

Don't Dwell on Mistakes

Jack used to joke that if he ever wrote a book about his experience, he would call it *Alibaba and the 1,001 Mistakes*. From watching Jack in action, I realized that two great traits every entrepreneur should possess are resilience and amnesia. In the face of setbacks Jack was incredibly resilient. And while I sometimes stewed over mistakes, Jack was so forward looking that he often forgot about the mistakes altogether. Mistakes are a by-product of success, to be learned from but not dwelled upon.

Embrace—Don't Run Away from— Tough Decisions

As a leader, it's impossible to please everyone. And even the most popular CEOs are not without their controversies. But leaders pioneering a business on a large scale are bound to face tough decisions, and it's important to face them head on and with conviction. This is something Jack had to learn over time, as he transitioned from being an English teacher to being a CEO. In 2000, as our company grew out of control, Jack was slow to make the layoffs necessary to save the company, choosing baby steps instead. It only worsened the problem and the company nearly went out of business which would have ended the employment of everyone in the company. After postponing the inevitable, we finally made the layoffs, stabilized the company, and grew on to hire many of the laid-off employees back. "I finally learned that sometimes I need to say 'no,'" Jack told me.

Have the Team Work for the Goal, Not for the Boss

Many traditional managers, especially in Asia, have top-down management styles. The boss issues directives and the employees focus their energies on pleasing the boss. And usually the boss is quite happy with that. But in Alibaba's case Jack set a high goal and then encouraged his team to chase the goal.

It helped keep everyone focused while minimizing the political infighting that often comes when employees spend most of their energy trying to please the boss.

Don't Disregard the "Tech Dummies"

Many people find it strange that an English teacher with no technical background could create the world's largest e-commerce company, especially when so many Internet start-ups are created by engineers. When I left Alibaba in 2008, Jack Ma could use a computer only for email and to use a browser. "Alibaba survived because I know nothing about technology," Jack would often say.

Jack's experience showed that being a self-professed "tech dummy" can be an asset for a manager in a consumer-oriented technology company. Whenever Alibaba's engineering team would prepare to introduce a new product, Jack would sit down for a sort of "Jack Ma dummy test." If Jack couldn't use it, he assumed the customer couldn't understand it. The approach worked. By keeping our websites simple, we stayed close to our customers, many of whom were using the Internet for the first time.

Don't Let It Get Personal

Meg Whitman made the mistake of letting eBay's competition with Alibaba get too personal. Once we got under her skin, eBay focused too much on the competition, and she and her team lost sight of the real goal—creating a great website for

China's consumers. Jack made the same mistake in our battle with former Yahoo! China head, Zhou Hongyi, and Yahoo! China's strategy veered off course.

ON BUILDING A SUCCESSFUL TEAM

Assemble a Team, Not a Collection of All-Stars

In 2000, in preparation for eventually having an IPO, Alibaba. com assembled a dream team of managers with pedigrees from Ivy League schools and leading multinationals and consulting firms. Their resumes would have looked great on a company prospectus, but the individuals didn't work well together. Their egos got in the way, and soon the company was adrift, headed dangerously close to bankruptcy. When this dream team was laid off, management reverted to the original founders. Although there were no all-stars among this team, they worked well together, achieving more together than someone might have predicted from their individual resumes.

Gather the Entire Team Once a Year

Alibaba is somewhat known in China for the massive all-hands meetings it held for its employees at the start of every year. Starting with a small party for the entire staff in 2000, the company continued to bring together all of its employees every year for an annual kick-off event, until it eventually required a stadium to seat the entire staff. As the company grew from 100 employees to 10,000, we gathered together staff from all around the world in Hangzhou for several days of speeches, activities, and team building exercises.

Bringing the entire team to Hangzhou was an expensive proposition for the company. But aligning everyone to the company's annual goals proved to be an important key to success for our fast-growing company. Company speeches and videos reminded everyone of where we'd come from in the previous year and set out a vision for where we'd be headed in the year ahead. And team building activities allowed staff members to catch up with old friends while building relationships across the organization.

Spread the Wealth

One of the key things that sets Alibaba apart from many of the start-ups I've come across is just how broadly Jack Ma shared Alibaba's ownership with employees through equity and stock options. The natural tendency for investors and company founders is to want to reserve stock incentives for only those in senior management positions. But starting with how he shared the equity broadly with his 17 cofounders, Jack continued to make sure that staff at all levels of the company were granted, or at least were eligible to earn through performance, stock options. In fact, when Alibaba.com went public in 2007, the company had to rent an arena to gather all of the staff holding stock options to walk them through the process for exercising their stock shares.

I strongly believe that Alibaba's team was driven by the idealistic goal of creating a platform that created opportunities for small businesses and entrepreneurs. But there can be no doubt that the shared sense of ownership helped unify the team to weather some tough storms together. We always knew that, if we did well for our customers we'd also share in the economic rewards. Having a broad-based sense of shared ownership helped unify the team.

Integrate Values into the Company's HR Systems

It's one thing to paste company values on a wall. It's another thing to codify the values into performance reviews. By tying 50 percent of an employee's bonus and advancement to values and 50 percent to performance, Alibaba was able to preserve its "Hupan culture" as it outgrew its apartment in Hupan Gardens and became a company with more than 25,000 employees.

Remember: Actions Speak Louder Than Words

As an MBA working in a Chinese start-up, I had to unlearn a lot of big-company tendencies, which favor analysis over action. At times I was bogged down in analyzing a strategy, and Jack would push me into action, chiding me by saying, "I won't fault you for making a mistake, but I will fault you for doing nothing." Getting into the game and trying something is more important than risking analysis paralysis.

Don't Judge a Growing Company by a Snapshot—Look at the Overall Trends

One of the toughest tasks for a manager in a start-up is to integrate new employees coming in from larger, more mature companies. The natural instinct for any new employee who has never worked in a start-up is to notice all the problems at the start-up that didn't exist at his former employer. One new employee with this attitude can be a challenge, as he often has buyer's remorse and privately begins to doubt his decision to join the company. But a group of new employees joining at the same time and having the same complaints can create a toxic environment.

It's important for new employees to understand that if someone were to take a snapshot from one day in the company, they would find a lot of problems. But if they stack those snapshots together over time and flip through them, they can see a trend of constant improvement.

Over time Alibaba recognized the importance of providing one to two weeks of orientation for new employees. They watched videos and attended speeches by the company managers that told the history of the company. This helped put an often messy one-day snapshot into its proper context and perspective.

Allow for Sabbaticals

A big problem in start-up companies is burnout. Staffers often work long hours and set aside personal interests for several years out of dedication to the cause. But companies should recognize that employees need time to recharge. And fast-growing companies need employees who have been a part of their early days to recharge and return to the company refreshed. I was fortunate that Jack was flexible and allowed me take a year off to pursue my dream of traveling around the world. When

I came back, I was fully recharged and determined to take on the world.

Be Sure to Hire the Right People at the Right Time

It's a cultural dilemma nearly every start-up faces—"When do we bring in the professional managers?" The risk-loving, fast-moving employee working out of an apartment is often a very different type of person than a seasoned manager working in a multinational. Both personalities are necessary in the life of a 102-year company, but when the two personalities collide, the result often is conflict and resentment.

In 2000 when Alibaba hired a team of senior international experts to manage the company, the resulting organizational disaster created a huge rift in the company. It was like plugging a Rolls Royce jet engine into a small hang glider. At the time we failed to recognize that a start-up needs people to serve as cultural bridges.

One bridge is a layer of people who can help carry the company from start-up to maturity. These are people who are flexible enough to work in an apartment but skilled enough to manage companies on a larger scale as they grow.

Alibaba needed an additional bridge, one that would help us "go global" and close the cultural gap between China and the West. In those early days the staff members who had Chinese-language skills and cultural understanding turned out to be a better fit than the staff members who had deep industry experience but little experience in China.

Honor and Respect the Work of
People Who Came Before You

In 2003 I was put in charge of Alibaba.com's international English-language website. It was the first time that a native English speaker was in charge of the site, and it wasn't hard to find several mistakes and features on the site that were not Westerner friendly.

My first move as a manager was to revamp the site's look and feel. I unveiled the new site at a meeting and put it up against the old site to show off what I had done and subtly point out what I viewed as the shabbiness of the site I had inherited. While my boss liked the presentation, I later realized that I should have done more to honor the work my colleagues had put into the previous site.

A start-up company is like a relay race: you carry the baton for a while and hand it off to the next person to improve it even more. There's no need to belittle the work that got the team this far. It's fun to look back on how far you've come and know that you carried the baton for a while.

ON DOING BUSINESS IN CHINA

Recognize That Innovation Is
Alive and Well in China

There seems to be a running narrative about tech entrepreneurs in China: the Chinese are great imitators but not great innovators. I've even heard it said that Alibaba is simply a copy of eBay. But that's like saying Steve Jobs copied the idea for the iPhone from Alexander Graham Bell. Alibaba's ecosystem in many ways bears no resemblance to that of eBay or Amazon.

While it is true that some sectors in China's economy are led by imitators, in many ways I found my colleagues and industry peers in China to be even more entrepreneurial than our counterparts in Silicon Valley. China's rapidly changing and dynamic market leads to a more nimble breed of entrepreneur. The Chinese also have a tremendous hunger for knowledge, education, and self-improvement—the result of so much human potential held in deep freeze for so long.

Channel Your Inner Taoist

It took eight years at Alibaba for me to fully appreciate the deep cultural differences that shape the management styles of Chinese entrepreneurs and their Western counterparts. In business school I was taught to approach a decision by gathering all relevant data and submitting them to rigorous frameworks and analysis before making a long-term plan. But at Alibaba I often found that this style was at odds with the approach of my colleagues, and I had to adjust to fit in. Over time I developed instincts for anticipating and smoothly adjusting to the company's frequent strategic changes and simply going with the flow.

When I joined Alibaba, Jack was criticized for publicly claiming, "At Alibaba we don't plan." And over time I realized that the majority of Jack's decisions were borne of gut instinct rather than deep analysis. Such an instinct-driven management style would drive just about any MBA crazy. And judging by the high turnover rate of my early Western colleagues, it often did.

Only upon reflection, after I left Alibaba, did I realize there were deeper cultural forces at work, namely, the influence of Taoist thinking on the culture of my colleagues and the company. According to the Taoist concept of Wu Wei, action should not involve excessive struggle that goes against the flow of nature. For example, water has a natural flow as it passes over rigid rocks and should not be diverted.

When Chinese and Western management styles come together, the Chinese management style resembles flowing water, whereas the Western management style resembles the rocks. Alibaba operated at the confluence of two dynamic forces—China and the Internet. Because of this we had to move and adapt quickly to changes in the industry and changes in China. In such an entrepreneurial market, going with the flow like water was much more important than sitting standing in the water's way like a rock.

Move First, Ask for Forgiveness Later

China is a rapidly changing market whose rules and regulations are constantly evolving. The leading companies don't sit on the sidelines and wait for the government regulators to make their position 100 percent clear. It's a delicate navigation, but in certain situations entrepreneurs have to move first and seek forgiveness later.

eBay sat on the sidelines as Alibaba introduced AliPay and therefore fell behind on online payments. Had eBay come up with a creative structure for its business, as Alibaba did, eBay could have found a way to enter the market.

Moving into a regulatory gray area should of course be constrained by moral, legal, and ethical considerations. But laws and regulations are made by humans and often were written before the era of the Internet. So at times companies need to push the regulatory frontier in order to deliver a service that has social benefits.

Love the Government but Don't Marry It

Government relations can be tricky, especially in environments with high levels of corruption, such as China. In such environments companies all too often think that the only way to motivate government officials is with bribes or kickbacks. But government officials can be motivated by a number of things, one of which is demonstrating to their constituents or bureaucratic superiors that they have done a positive thing for their city, province, or country.

Alibaba recognized this, and we set out to make our home city, Hangzhou, the center of e-commerce innovation in China. To this end we organized high-level conferences of world leaders and business people that put Hangzhou on the map as a sort of Silicon Valley in Paradise. The media attention became a self-fulfilling prophesy, and before long Alibaba was seen as a model company in the city. This had the dual benefit of making government officials happy while protecting us from bureaucrats looking for kickbacks.

Loving the government doesn't mean you have to love all the government's policies. And in today's tricky environment it's hard to imagine that Western businesses will love and embrace the Chinese government's policies every step of the way. The more important point is don't marry the government—getting too close to the government is a risk for any company. The best approach to government relations is simply to do the right thing for your customers, employees, and community and make sure people are aware of your good deeds.

Remember: The Most Important *Guanxi* Is with Your Customer

Back in the 1980s the talk among all foreign business people operating in China was about how to establish the best *guanxi*—relationships—with local government officials who could help businesses enter China's highly regulated market. But as China opened, the economy became much more of a meritocracy.

Early foreign entrants in China's Internet industry would boast about their relationships with high-level government officials. And when eBay handed over its local business to a relative of the Hong Kong tycoon Li Ka-shing, it made the mistake of thinking that guanxi alone could solve its problems. Getting the door open is important, but it no longer ensures success.

In China's highly competitive market—just like everywhere else—the guanxi that matters most to a company's future is its relationships with customers.

NOTES

CROCODILE IN THE YANGTZE

1. "EBAY—eBay 2005 Analyst Day," transcript by Thomson StreetEvents, February 10, 2005.

THE EBAY-ALIBABA HOTLINE

1. Ina Steiner, "eBay Live 2005 Conference Wrap-Up," EcommerceBytes. com, July 10, 2005.

THE DEAL HEARD 'ROUND THE WORLD

1. *Crocodile in the Yangtze: The Alibaba Story* (documentary film), directed by Porter Erisman, Taluswood Films, 2012.
2. Peter S. Goodman, "Yahoo Says It Gave China Internet Data," *Washington Post,* September 11, 2005.

WINTER

1. Gady Epstein, "Alibaba's Jack Ma Fights to Win Back Trust," *Forbes,* March 23, 2011.

ALIBABA'S WORLD

1. Liu Yi and Sophie Yu, "Alibaba's Founder Jack Ma Turns to Pursuing Cultural Endeavours," *South China Morning Post,* July 13, 2013.

INDEX